Inspire A
Teacher Within

Inspire A

Teacher Within

Because everyone is a
learner to a Teacher...

Dr. Ashok Patel
(Ph.D)

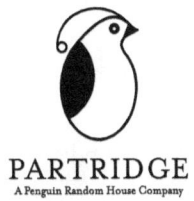

PARTRIDGE
A Penguin Random House Company

To order additional copies of this book, contact
Partridge India
000 800 10062 62
orders.india@partridgepublishing.com

www.partridgepublishing.com/india

CONTENTS

FOREWORD

Dr.Ashok Patel is an eminent educationist and is a teacher educator par excellence. On account of his creative and communicative capabilities he was invited to write weekly educational column in 'Sandesh' which is one of the oldest daily newspapers in Gujarat State. The column entitled 'Kelavani na Kinare' has become very popular and is widely read.

Through this column, Dr. Patel has shared his perceptive observations and experiences with educators, parents and the public at large on a variety of interesting and enlightening educational topics. Out of a large number of themes that he has dealt with during the past 7 years, he has selected 26 titles specially pertaining to teachers for preparing this valuable book.

There has always been a perennial question: "Who is a successful teacher?" This issue is examined for millennia in India and abroad by different cultures and civilizations. But the answer to it is neither static nor constant; it changes with time due to the waves of changes in society, economy, philosophy, psychology, technology and such other forces. Dr.Patel has ventured in his columns, besides other literature that he has produced, to examine various characteristic features of an effective and committed teacher. I am happy to state that his venture in this critical aspect of education and human development has become highly successful especially in the context of contemporary scenario of school and colleges in the 21st century. What is more, he has presented his ideas and experiences under pithy and catchy titles in order to attract the attention of readers. Dr.Patel's characteristic style of generating catchy titles of his columns is both interesting and thought-provoking. " The Teacher Should Be a Theist and Not an Atheist." is just one example that makes us think and attract us to critically read what the learned author says on this type of an ambivalent, if not a controversial, issue in a so-called secular society. Does secularism mean atheism? Every teacher and every citizen of India must understand this issue in depth, so that teachers can succeed in building a synthesis between India's rich heritage and cultural continuity on the one hand and techno-based global modernization on the other.

In recent decades, the field of education is fast expanding in Gujarat and India. In Gujarat, for example, there are more than 50,000 Anganwadis where more than a lakh of teachers are engaged in taking care of health and education of infants and children from 0 to 6. At the primary stage, from classes 1 to 8, there are some three lakhs of teachers educating children and early adolescents from age 6 to 14, under the new law of R.T.E.. Likewise, at the secondary stage, the project entitled Rashtriya Madhyamik Shiksha Abhiyan (RMSA), started in March 2009 on a national scale aspires for the goal of near- universalization of secondary education. Thus the number of teachers and principals are swelling by leaps and bounds at the secondary and higher secondary stage. At the stage of higher education also, the aim of the current 12th Five Year Plan is to add one crore more learner during the plan period raising the Gross Enrolment Ratio

(GER) from 18% to about 25% in the second decade of the current century. In Gujarat alone the number of universities has increased from 10 to 45 in about one decade.

All these developments indicate that there are increasingly more teachers and principals who have to tackle the problems of expansion of education at all stages and concurrently raise quality, creativity, value-orientation practical skills and excellence. In this context, the present book is extremely valuable in progressing towards this goal.

Therefore, for focussing this book on teachers and principals based on weekly blogs, Dr.Ashok Patel deserves our heartfelt appreciation. I trust that the book will be useful not only to teachers and principals, but to teacher educators, teacher-trainees and others involved in the field of education. I wish the book a great success.

Ahmedabad   Prof. (Dr.) R.H.Dave

21-01-2015   Former Director, UNESCO, Germany

PREFACE

Education is my cup of tea. Experimenting in the field of education has become a real treasure for me. Hence writing articles on educational system, teacher's special work in the classroom and the responsibility of the principal in the institute are the main subjects to be delineated at various levels. I went through different experiences in the educational field working as a school teacher in primary section, as a professor in educational college and holding the responsibility as a member of Educational Committee of secondary & higher secondary education board in Gujarat state. As the years passed by I had come in contacts with the motivators, educationalist, bureaucrats and real lovers of education at large. Sometimes the bliss of being in educational field enriched me but sometimes despair also clouded me. Through my writings I presented certain issues to be taken care of, certain problems to be solved soon and certain matters of appreciation to be rejoiced.

Different experiences shocked me and I started writing about them with the hope to have changes in the present scenario. Going through the value based educational system I found that certain teachers and principals have tried their best to bring about drastic changes in their schools and in the surrounding societies, They have become the role models for students and the guardians. To promote overall development of the child we have good institutes, but we lack the commitment to fulfil our goals because of teacher's irresponsibility, lack of interest, devotion and teaching skill.

My intention in creating the awareness among the people connected with educational field has come up with the current issues, incidents and occurrences. To enable the teacher and principal to encourage the students, my articles would be penetrating on the practical aspect, on the human approach and better utilization of the government sources. It is the universal understanding that education helps a child to be a perfect citizen in society. Education never enhances sorrow or disparity; it never discourages anybody or never brings about negative changes. On the contrary education means a successful and blissful society created by the learned citizens with wisdom and knowledge where the generations of different people live in peace and harmony and work for the progress of the nation.

I wish from the bottom of my heart that the readers would join hands to bring about at least one positive change in the field of education and it will be my real achievement in writing on education. I am hopeful that the teachers and the principals will have the thought provoking process for the true success in education.

Dr.Ashok Patel (Ph.D. in Education)

(Residing)

Associate professor,   21-A Vidhata Society,

S.U.G. College of Education,   K.K. Nagar Road – Ghatlodia,

Vasna-Ahmedabad - 380007   Ahmedabad – 380061

Gujarat–India   Gujarat - India

Mobile : +919426004542

Email : dr.ashokpatel@gmail.com

www.learnandteach.in

1

TEACHER SHOULD BE A THEIST NOT AN ATHEIST

*A*ccording to the dictionary, a theist means the believer in the existence of God and the other world. Besides, it also means a confiding person, from this point of view a teacher must be a devout person. The question is: In which case should the teacher be confiding? In whom should he have faith?

First of all, the teacher should have confidence in himself. How would other persons have faith on the person who lacks self-confidence himself? The teacher has to view himself a little higher and dignified in his demeanor. He should have ample self-confidence. Only then, the students as well as the guardians / parents will repose confidence or trust in him. The teacher filled with self-confidence always endears himself to the students, guardians, co-teachers, and the society. All his deeds are interesting and are easily acceptable. He is loved by all. Such meritorious person is always successful. The basic requirement for this is to know himself, his strengths, and limitations.

Secondly, he must have faith in his work. This is not at all difficult for the teacher who knows himself very well. He must have deep faith in whatever work or activity that he undertakes in classroom, school or society. The teacher who is doubtful whether his work or activity will be successful or not, will never succeed. His character must be good and beyond suspicion. He must positively attempt to do his work with the confidence to reach the zenith of success. How would the students and the guardians have trust in his work or activities, when he himself lacks trust and confidence in his own work? The work begun with full sincerity will meet with success on its own. Failure perchance would be only in our interest. It may be a lesson to learn for us. We believe that the person who learns as well as teaches is the teacher. Thus the teacher has, not only to teach but to learn, for. Thus, irrespective of success or failure in a teacher's work, the victory belongs to the teacher alone.

Thirdly, the teacher should have faith on and trust in his students. If you do not have deep faith on those with whom you have to work, they will neither have faith on you nor in your work. Hence have full faith on the students as if they are your sons and behave with them accordingly. Some teachers are often heard, remarking, "These students are quite weak, irregular, lazy and dull they come to school not to learn, but they come because their parents/guardians push them to school". Then the question arises: suppose that they come to school, not for learning, but how about you as a teacher? Do you not go to school for teaching? Then begin to teach them. The teacher's tendency reflected in his remarks about the students would never help him to become successful as a teacher. Hence it is essential that the teacher should trust and have respect for his students, their capabilities, their environment, and heritage. In this context, he has to organize his teaching techniques and methods. The trust reposed by the teacher in students regarding their capabilities serves as an inspiration to them to win new summits.

Every student has an inner desire that he would like to become his teacher's favorite student. This could be possible only when the teacher and the students are close to one another. Such proximity is possible only when the teacher begins to trust the student. The greater the proximity (closeness) between the teacher and the taught, the higher is the achievement of the taught (student).

In view of the position cited above, the teacher should be confident in three aspects: (a) himself (b) his work and (c) the students. He should have faith in God. The teacher who has faith in God, tries to please God by discharging his duty sincerely. Generally it is found that the person believing in god has deep down faith in god. An atheist has ample leisure, which makes him purposeless and evil-minded. Thus it is in the interest of teaching as well as education that the teacher should not be an atheist but he should be a theist (believer in God). The teacher's intention is to make the students enjoy his learning. Slowly the teacher has to spread the sheet of faith and make the students take interest in education. Atheism is the sister of vanity. An atheist enjoys talking ill will. It is better for education that these vices should never enter the psyche of the teacher. Atheism is considered to be the first step of failure.

Note:

- *Every student has an inner desire that he would like to become his teacher's favorite student. This could be possible only when the teacher and the students are close to one another.*
- *The teacher should be confident in three aspects: (a) himself (b) his work and (c) the students.*

2

SMILEY TEACHER LOOKS GOOD

The writer who is the Professor of Education was observing a student-teacher's (trainees) lesson in a school. She was a lady. Her style of speaking was good. The Professor constantly felt that something was lacking. It was the smile that she lacked. Had she given the lesson with a smile on her face, it would have been more enjoyable, during that moment the teacher's face seems to be uglier than that of a fiend or an ogre. Why should the teacher remain aloof with such a face? Such teachers are far off from the student's heart. In her observation note book, I remarked, "A smiling teacher appears good in complexion." There was a group discussion with that lady. All student-teachers felt that the teacher with a serious face does not look good at all. Nobody would prefer him. Excessive seriousness tends to increase the distance between the students and the teacher. The more the distance, the less is the communication between them.

A teacher's job is not limited to the teaching only, but to encourage the student to learn too. In my view, the latter is more important than the former. In other words, encouraging students to learn is more important than teaching them. If the student is encouraged to learn, he will, of course, learn in presence of the teacher. Not only then, but he will continue to learn even in his absence also. He will learn very much on his own. To make the student learn by himself is the real process of education. But in today's classroom the majority of teachers believe that if they teach, then only they know what to do and how to do it. As against this, compared to what you teach, they know more than what you have not taught them. Hence come out of that misunderstanding that if you teach, then only they learn. The teacher's real function is to give guidance. Let the student do himself; learn himself. Done in this way, he will remember for long the knowledge or wisdom thus achieved. It will be very useful to him also. Inspire the students to learn on their own accord. Words alone would not inspire them; even the words with reasoning would not help. The students would accept with trust what you say with smiling face only.

If the teacher teaches in the classroom with smiling face, the students will consider him as more familiar. They would like to talk with him or ask him. They would feel free to present before him their needs, problems, or confusion. In this way, the teaching-learning process will become natural. Smiling becomes a short and simple way to enter into the heart of the individual in front of you. The teacher remaining detached from the students would never be able to teach them anything. To teach or inspire students, the teacher has to reach their hearts and attract them to his own heart. For this purpose, only the natural smile on face would be useful. Approach with smile the student who could not answer the question, and try to encourage him. You will surely find a great change in him in a few moments. Even if he may not know the correct answer to the teacher's question, he would try to reply. The teacher's smiling face would encourage even the silent learner to respond orally.

During the school time the students would be approaching the teacher with some work or problem, small or big. At that time, some teachers would be harsh in behaviour with them without listening to them fully. They would even threaten them. Such teachers would avoid meeting the students. They would even take pride in declaring, "See, no student dares to meet me!" Such teachers should retire as early as possible in students' interest as well as in the interest of education. When any student approaches the teacher, he should welcome him with the smiling face, listen to him and then give him his opinion. The student will, probably, accept his opinion with smiling face even if he may not like it. The teacher should smile but not laugh at him. He should also see that the student may not try to befool him.

The teacher is also a socially responsible person. Hence he may also have to face economic as well as social problems. He should be on his guard and mature enough to see that those problems do not affect the school environment. Otherwise, the students would know about them from your face and discuss about the same with their friends or parents (guardians) without fail. Thus the students are the real canvasser of the teacher's personality. Hence, it is necessary that the teacher should keep his problems limited to himself only. The day when he feels that he is beset with problems, it is beneficial to stay at home that day on leave rather than report on duty that day with gloomy face. Smiling is, so to say, a teaching technique on account of which the teacher can bring about positive change among students easily. To bring about such change when the teacher enters the school or the classroom, how could he afford to do so without having the educational device in the form of 'Smile'? The teacher has to keep the teaching aid i.e. 'smile' in his pocket all the time which is ever useful in the class room, in the staff room, on the ground or meeting with the guardian.

If the teacher teaches in the classroom with smiling face, the students will consider him as more familiar.

Note:

- *To make the student learn by himself is the real process of education.*
- *To teach or inspire students, the teacher has to reach their hearts and attract them to his own heart. For this purpose, only the natural smile on face would be useful.*

3

TEACHER'S JOB IS NOT ONLY TO SAY, BUT TO HEAR

*I*n the classroom the teacher and the students interact with one another. During the interaction, the activity on both the sides is not only necessary but inevitable. Inaction (or inactivity) of any one side works as a bump for the achievement of the objective. Hence the classroom environment should be so created as would encourage constant interaction between the teacher and the students as well as among the students themselves. To achieve this objective, it is the teacher who is the source of inspiration as well as the creator of the favorable classroom environment.

Let us think over the present-day classroom situation. The child-learner is found alive in the classroom with suffocating voice, but its meaning is understood differently: The teacher is the king and the students are his soldiers. Just as the king's order is to be followed by the soldiers, with complete obedience to the king, the class room king has to be obeyed by the student without argument. How can such a class be considered a heaven? Today's classroom seems to be a hell instead of a heaven.

The teacher is considered to be generally the king of his classroom. The students have got to obey him silently. The sooner we come out of such a closed situation, the better it would be for the learners' and the society's welfare.

Sometime we hear the teachers saying, that the students do not pay attention to what they say. They turn deaf ears to what we instruct. They have become self-willed. Then the desire to counter-question cannot be stopped. To what extent do you (as teacher) listen to them or their desires? The others would listen to them who pay attention to them. As you sow, so shall you reap. You are respected, if you respect others. We may call it the teacher's duty to fulfil the students' expectations from the teachers before getting his expectations fulfilled by the students.

The students must have enough freedom to present their voice in or outside the classroom and for that purpose there must be the amicable environment prevalent in the school. Let the students present their difficulties freely. Adopt the positive attitude to listen to them. Certain robust teachers should be advised not to intimidate the students. The teacher is expected to build up sincere relationship with a living individual – a student. If both the parties do not have respect or faith for one another, no mental relationship would ever be built up. This would adversely affect the teaching – learning process. During the day the student is required to discuss or present various matters with the teacher. At that time the teacher should encourage him and take part in the discussion with him. He should listen to such students, encourage them and take part in the discussion with them. The learning process is operative only when the learner is comfortable and is in a position to present his difficulties and is able to get the solution. During the teaching process, he should very often ask questions to the learners and encourage them to learn through counter-questioning. If the student cannot speak or is not able to express his views on account of the teacher's awe or authority, that teacher can be called an unsuccessful teacher. During the teaching process, the teacher should create such a congenial classroom environment as would encourage the students to speak, ask and know as much as possible. As the teacher goes to the school or the college to teach, so also the students enter to learn. Both the parties have right to speak as well as the duty to listen to one another. The mutual discussion or talk between the students – learners during classroom teaching process should be taken as a positive phenomenon.

When the two students are found talking with each other while the teacher is teaching, their discussion might be pertaining to their non-understanding of the subject-matter, his way of teaching and so on. It is, therefore, essential that the teacher should approach such students and try to understand their difficulty and solve it. Under such classroom situation, the teacher should refrain from becoming stern and avoid using indecent language for either the students or their parents. He should not inflict punishment.

Every human being has been always thinking about something or the other. He might also be trying to give expression to his thoughts. As we know teaching is a reflective process, and all of us do acknowledge it. As we have freedom to think, we should also have freedom to speak. The more the permissive and free atmosphere of the classroom, the more degree of classroom interaction would be between the teacher and the learners as well as among the learners themselves.

With a view to making the classroom a paradise for learning, let the students speak and interact to the maximum extent. The teacher who speaks to the minimum extent and allows the students to speak and express themselves to the maximum extent is indeed a good and real teacher. Thus the teacher is not expected to go on telling only, but he has to listen to what the students have to say or express. The person who listens to others would also be listened to by others.

Note:

- *The learning process is operative only when the learner is comfortable and is in a position to present his difficulties and is able to get the solution.*
- *The teacher who speaks to the minimum extent and allows the students to speak and express themselves to the maximum extent is indeed a good and real teacher.*

4

THE TEACHER SHOULD SHOW DEVOTION, NOT RULE

The function of schools and colleges is to cultivate values along with imparting education. In this regard, the society and the government have some expectations from the schools, colleges and the teachers. For the fulfilment thereof, specific rules and regulations are made. Notwithstanding this, full satisfaction is lacking. Are the rules and regulations not adequate? What is lacking in the absence of which the expected goal is not reached? It is nothing but Devotion. In case of teachers, what is important? Rule or Devotion?

Based on experience it can be concluded that if there is devotion, the rules will naturally be observed. But it cannot be stated with certainty that devotion will be the outcome of the observance of the rules. Hence devotion is given predominance over rules. Devotion can bring out change in a person's thinking as well as behaviour, whereas the rules bring out change in behaviour only. It is, therefore, necessary to have congenial environment in the classroom, as well as devotion on the part of the teacher for imparting comprehensive education.

It is not enough to have knowledge based cognitive relationship only between the student and the teacher. It is much more necessary to have emotional relationship between the two. For example, take the case of an ill child who would not take medicine even if the parents fondle him and request him? On the contrary, the same child would be prepared to have it at the request of the teacher. This itself indicates that for the child (or say, learner) who is studying in school, the teacher is held in high esteem.

Likewise, a collegian seeking guidance on selection of an occupation for a career would accept the right suggestion or guidance of the professor. If the teacher or the lecturer says that his duty is restricted only to the timings of the school or the college, it is not in accordance with the Indian ideology. If the teacher is devoted to his profession as well as to the students, he will be engrossed in such work or activity that would be in the interest of the students as well as education.

It is a rule that the teacher should be punctual to reach the school. On his way to school, he finds a child facing some problem. He helps the child; as a result he is late in reporting for duty. In such circumstances, the Principal tells the teacher with anger, "Let the child come, whatever the situation! It is not our duty to help the child on way; it is his/her parent's duty. You must come to school in time. Here we find a conflict between rule and devotion. Which of the two is more important? A science teacher teaches a lesson on: Sky observation. He believes that actually the sky observation can be undertaken only at night. But the schools are closed at night. The students cannot be asked to come to school at night. His duty hours are from 11 a.m. to 5 p.m. only;

whereas another teacher invites the students either at school or some definite place along with the parents/guardians and conducts 'sky observation'. Which out of these two situations is acceptable?

With a view to creating educational environment in schools and colleges, organization of co-curricular activities is of great importance. If teaching is to be restricted to the text-books only, then it is not necessary to start the four-walled schools and colleges and to expend financially after building up the four-walled structures of schools and colleges. With the help of books as guides, the teacher has to fulfil manifold objectives. For this, only the text-book and rules would not be sufficiently effective. What is needed is the whole-hearted devotion and dedication on the part of the teachers. The Principal cannot frame rules for teachers to give extra time to teach very poor students. If he dares to do so, the teacher may not observe such rules. A teacher with devotion would sincerely try to help the students in their study, either prior to the commencement of school time or even after the school time is over. By rule, you can create office type atmosphere, but not at all like a family.

Teaching is not an activity only of brain, but of heart also. If you want to initiate heart also in that activity, the rule will be of no importance. For that purpose, everybody must build up faith in human resources. The teacher also needs to reach not only the child's brain, but the heart also. For this purpose, if the rules need to be ignored, let it be so. Only devotion should be predominant.

The teacher, who makes it a rule that he should teach only the text-book, may impart knowledge, but not values. Knowledge alone is not useful in social life; values are more essential. The teachers having only knowledge are nothing but the moving books! Therefore, uses of heart rather than brain and devotion rather than rule are more expected from the teacher. It is not necessary to believe that the teacher bestowed with knowledge would impart it fully to the learners. He may even, state: I impart knowledge that I have to the learners in the classroom. But what can I do if they do not grasp it? On the other hand, the devoted teacher feels happy to impart necessary and useful information and knowledge to the learners. He does so with sincerity and full devotion, using necessary technique and method. On the other hand, the teacher possessing only knowledge would be satisfied with the feeling that the period of teaching is over.

Thus, for a teacher devotion is of immense importance compared to knowledge and rule. If there is devotion, everything else will be available on its own. Hence the teacher should show devotion rather than rule, the result of which would be beneficial for all concerned.

Note:

> *Devotion can bring out change in a person's thinking as well as behaviour, whereas the rules bring out change in behaviour only.*

> *Knowledge alone is not useful in social life; values are more essential.*

5

THE TEACHER'S SUCCESS IS THE STUDENT'S SUCCESS

The main aim of a teacher is to lead the student also to success. Such success should be concerned with manifold aspects of life. It is the mark of incomplete education, if a student successful in one or two aspects is found weak in other aspects of learning. The main aim of education is considered to lead to the all-round development of the student. Who can help the student achieve such success? Naturally, this is possible if he is fortunate to have a good teacher. Good teacher implies successful teacher - successful in various aspects like teaching, education and living. Such teacher inspires the student community through his experience and illustrations, finally leading to the peak of success. Whom shall we call a successful teacher? The teacher, who is a source of inspiration for the students, parents/guardians, school and the society concerned, can be called the successful teacher.

The distinguishing characteristics of the teacher who is capable of leading the students to the successful achievement through the classroom teaching are as follows:

- His classroom teaching is effective.
- He is innovative in his approach to teaching.
- He keeps the students busy with learning and joyful activities.
- His absence of even one day is not liked by the students.
- He becomes one with the students forgetting his own self.
- He is committed to the student's welfare.
- He shares his good and benign experiences with the students.

The teacher with such distinguishing characteristics endears himself to the students, and this result in the achievement of the mutual goal of successful career.

Compared to his age, the student today learns very much. The environment helps him with the result that he begins knowing the teacher in a very short span of time. Only thereafter, he gets either impressed or not by the teacher. The student today wants to be successful in multifarious aspects of life. In such a case, he wants a teacher who would be a good guide, or say, a role model. Such teacher would be competent enough to help him achieve his goal. Hence the challenge before the teacher is that he should recognize the student of today, and know his needs. He shall have to satisfy these needs. It is not enough that he is proficient in classroom transaction. The teacher can be a source of inspiration for the students, only when he is successful in various aspects of life. The student today likes a modern teacher as also the one who is insistent for good values. He also likes that teacher who can sing well, play well and operate computer very well. The teacher having a good 'mobile/cell phone' is also liked by the students. Such teacher impresses the students mind positively.

The teacher who is successful in the classroom cannot be called a perfectly successful teacher in the true sense. The teacher is not concerned only with the classroom. Had it been so, the society would not be celebrating 'Teacher's Day'. He would not have been called the social guard. Together with the classroom, he has to succeed in the society also by performing his proper role in it, as an inspiring and motivating person. The teacher who is constantly trying to lead the community to a positive direction in the changing world is regarded with respect and trust.

The teacher who enjoys the trust and confidence of the parents of guardians becomes easily trustworthy in the society. The only expectation of the parent/guardian from the teacher is that he imparts good education and culture to the child - son or daughter. If he discharges his duty fully well in these two aspects, he will surely endear himself to the parents/guardians. In school the behaviour of the teacher with the guardians either brings him closer to them or keeps him at a distance. The teacher who cannot deal with the parents/guardians with love cannot be expected to invite them to their homes. Just think of the situation in the past when the parents/guardians used to bow down or salute the teachers of the olden times on way!

A teacher has a house to live in. He loves it and maintains it well. He tries to keep it up-to-date. Likewise he should try his best to make the school also well-adorned or elegant. He should take the development of the school as his own development. Only the teacher with vision and mission can contribute to the progressive development of the school. How deplorable it is when a teacher just forgets the school as soon as he leaves the school gate! It can be said that in the success of teacher lies the progress of the school.

To achieve overall success, it is necessary that, first of all, the teacher must be self-motivated; he must be proficient in teaching, he should keep himself up-to-date in activities such as, reading, writing, listening, discussing and going on excursions with the students and colleagues.

To be quick in updating knowledge and technology, the use of internet becomes helpful and effective tool. The teacher should aim at excellence in every aspect of work and living. In any case a weak and meek teacher is never liked by the student. He has to be the best in every sphere and show the same. Only that group of students can achieve success who is fortunate to have such successful teachers to guide them. Remember that it is a long and planned journey to become successful.

Note:

- *The teacher, who is a source of inspiration for the students, parents/guardians, school and the society concerned, can be called the successful teacher.*
- *It is a long and planned journey to become successful.*

6

LET THE TEACHERS MAKE THE ANTI - TERRORISM IDEOLOGY PROSPEROUS

*T*en years have passed since the terrorist attack on WORLD TRADE CENTRE, New York which took place on September 11, 2001. As a sequel to it, the United States of America declared war entitled: "Operation Enduring Freedom", against worldwide terrorism. It was a tragic coincidence with memorable lecture by Swami Vivekananda before the World Religion Congregation in Chicago on September 11, 1893. He had exhorted the audience for love and peace that are the essence of all religions of the world.

Today terrorism has become the subject of great concern for the entire world. There may rarely be any such country which might not have become a prey of terrorism. Terrorism is war against democracy and crime against humanity. The twentieth and the twenty-first centuries have become the centuries for new inventions, say, the countries of new technologies. (Unfortunately) the terrorism was also discovered and had been operational during this period of time. The technology that was to be used for human welfare is being used unfortunately for ruining human beings and properties. After Independence since 2003, 60000 and more people became the prey of terrorism in India It is regretful to note that innumerable persons and properties have become victim to terrorist attacks.

The targets of terrorists' attacks were:

- Destruction of US World Centre, Legislative Assembly of Jammu and Kashmir, Delhi Parliament Building.
- Attacks on Akshardham Building in Gandhinagar, Bomb Blast on Taj Hotel Building in Mumbai. Bomb Blasts on capital Riyadh of Saudi Arabia and in Morocco, Terrorists attacks in London... At present the terrorist's attacks even in Pakistan, the origin of terrorism, prove that the terrorism neither belongs to any country nor to any religion. Destruction, fear violence and physical as well as mental terror - these are what they call their religious duties.

There is little difference between revolt and terrorism. Revolt is limited only to the national boundary and it is in protest against their government. It is operative with the co-operation of the local community of their own country. Creation of Nagaland in India was due to the rebellious behaviour of the people. Assam state was also shaken with rebellious activities. A few days back, the rebels have abandoned violence on account of the settlement between them and the government. The disruptive activities of the naxalites can only be termed as the rebellion. Beginning from the naxalbari region of the West Bengal, it has spread to Orissa, Andhra Pradesh, Kerala, Tripura, Chattisgadh, Zarkhand and Madhya Pradesh, whereas terrorism has spread to the international states, it has no geographical boundaries. As we know, it is operative either against one's own country or against the government of another country. The terrorists kill a person and frighten many people. This can be termed as a psychological technique. When the terrorism is rampant, every country should teach its citizens from their childhood the ways and means to fight against it and put an end to it.

'Features of terrorism' have been included in the curricula of the schools and colleges. Our educationists have been trying to awaken the student's right from Class-8 on the issue of terrorism. We have a hunch that knowledge based awareness alone would not help eradicate terrorism. Compared to the vehemence and courage with which the terrorists are trying to terrorize people, will the students of today have courage to get prepared to confront terrorism? Are there such inspiring and encouraging leaders like Anna Hazare to exhort the students or the youth to fight against terrorism? Do the politicians have any effective way except public speech? Alas, the present day students or the youth have begun showing aversion or contempt towards politicians and their politics. This was clearly evident during the agitation against corruption. How much crippled our democracy or government has become that it takes too long to decide suitable punishment and then to execute it firmly! The present day youth does not like this: Politics even in punishing the terrorists! How strange it is when the regional government recommends waiving the punishment of hanging (to death) to the terrorists who killed Rajiv Gandhi! Today the state of rebellion or terrorism is prevalent in different states of India. How strange does it look when the governments concerned demand reduction or pardon the nature or the period of the punishment announced for the culprits! In such situation the selfish nature of the political party is unveiled. How far is it proper to discuss such political matters or decisions during the classroom teaching learning situation, as additional information? What would be the effect of this on the student's minds?

Politics would not work in fighting against terrorism. Teamwork may be useful. Definite and positive decisions must be executed. Immediate justice must be done. Much delayed justice is tantamount to only injustice. Extremely slow judicial process of ours in pronouncing justice needs to be hastened. We must guard ourselves against wrong decisions under the garment of human rights or democracy. But who would save whom from such situation? Political parties are more interested in personal politics rather than destroying terrorism. They are busy with finding faults of other political parties or they cannot spare time from saving corrupt or goonda-like persons of their party. In India terrorism has spread for the last 20-25 years. The main reason for its spread is that the terrorists find India safe for them to spread terrorism. In such hopeless situation, the people have only one alternative and that is to offer prayer to God: Oh God, give our political leaders such intellect and power so that they can fight against terrorism with sincerity. And also make the terrorists wise enough that they may shun terrorising activities. But till God does not listen to this prayer, the teachers should perform their roles sincerely and impartially to keep up anti terrorism line of thinking in the classroom.

Note:

When the terrorism is rampant, every country should teach its citizens from their childhood the ways and means to fight against it and put an end to it.

7

TEACHER DOES WHAT HE ASPIRES

*E*very individual likes to become a prominent person. This is a positive sign; but not all of them succeed in that dream. Teaching profession also is not an exception in such case. There can be two divisions of persons who desire to become teachers. First, such teachers who really wanted to become teachers, indeed, became teachers willingly. The others are those who became teachers even though they were not willing to become teachers. We must salute the teachers of the first category, whereas we have the second category of those teachers who became teachers even though they had no desire to become teachers. To them we must advise, "Now that you have indeed become teachers, you must perform your duty as teachers with full sincerity and nobility." Let me say that teaching is such a profession whereby you can get as much satisfaction as you wish and achieve development as well.

'Eat, drink and make merry' - Can this be the man's aim of life? As individuals differ, so their aims of life also differ. Since we are born in this world, it is our duty to dedicate something substantial to it. Let the society acknowledge it. Some persons take up service to community, some would like politics, some others would establish institutions for the welfare of the society and some prefer to be saintly persons. In my opinion, for social service and welfare, teaching profession is the best of all. Today many people blame the politicians and certain institute. There are so-called sadhus wondering from house to house to feed themselves or certain person having declared himself saint creates small group of devotees. Then it is reflected that the society would not be at loss if such persons had not become sadhus.

With the entry in youthfulness, the person should decide the goal of his life. Then he should try to reach the goal sincerely and tirelessly. Having achieved more development than others, he will be able to play a specific role in society. Today it is generally observed that a person selects his goal, works in that field of profession, but is not adequately satisfied, because he lacks either depth or innovativeness in his work. Consequently, he changes his way or field of work. In my view, such persons rarely succeed in the new field of work, because they might have completed nearly half span of active life. In the new field of work, he is required to know and learn afresh and also to get himself adjusted to the new situation of work.

It is in his interest that once he has entered upon the teaching profession, he must get himself engrossed in it with devotion. Ponder deeply that every year you teach one hundred students. Generally during 35 years 3500 students would learn. These numbers of students remember you because you have nurtured them with knowledge and wisdom. Even their parents do remember you for the whole life moreover if you prove to be a genius teacher, there would be thirty-five thousand people respecting you. When you happen to pass by the road or stand at the bus stop, certain person approaches you, bows to you and declares that he was your student. At this juncture your pleasure knows no bound even compared to winning a lottery ticket worth Rs. 5 lakh. The positive and everlasting impression of a good and clever teacher created on the minds of the learners is so strong that they will remember him throughout their life. Even the parents/guardians would never forget him.

A teacher can easily transmit his ideas, culture and beliefs to students. In doing so, he does great service to society. This is, in no way, inferior to the social service rendered by Sadhus and saints. There is no other profession except the teaching profession where everybody would greet you saying, 'Sir'. From peon to police chief, clerk to collector, or even secretary of state or Judge-all of them would call you 'Sir'. Are these illustrations not adequate to illustrate the greatness of the teaching profession?

What is it that a teacher cannot do? He can mar or make the government. 'Chanakya', a great politician and philosopher has affirmed, 'Teacher is never ordinary....!' A teacher can become a scientist as well as the President of the nation. The teacher can become a good orator, as well as a good musician also. He can become a good writer and good poet also. It is necessary for a teacher to know his capabilities, and develop them and use them for social welfare activities. Hence it is necessary to take positive decision: 'I want to become great by becoming a good teacher.'

Note:

- *'Teacher is never ordinary....!'*
- *For social service and welfare, teaching profession is the best of all.*

8

TEACHERS! ARISE, AWAKE AND STOP NOT TILL YOU ACHIEVE THE ULTIMATE KNOWLEDGE

The present century is not only a modern century, but it is progressing as an ultra-modern century. In this century, for better living, man needs to have the latest knowledge, besides air, water, food and shelter. The present century is progressing by leaps and bounds. With your snail's speed, you are bound to be pushed aside, unnoticed by anybody. Today every person is anxious to proceed further for self-development. To achieve this goal, he is prepared to do his level best. Under these circumstances, if the teacher who is concerned with imparting knowledge to the students fails to discharge his duty, he will not be accepted by the students of today or tomorrow.

Today the student in the classroom is not empty-headed. He possesses not only the domestic information, but he is also equipped with useful information about the world also. In his comfortable house, he can avail himself of the latest electronic appliances like TV, computer, cell phone, and what not. TV channels continuously provide him the treasure knowledge round the clock. Internet is available to help him locate and collect necessary and latest information about the subject he needs instantly.

The learner who do not possess the Internet facility, take resort to newspapers and periodicals to satisfy their interests. That is why the newspapers have to publish separate supplements. The child breathing in such atmosphere becomes not only the drop of knowledge but also the ocean of knowledge. Thus there are various ways for youngsters to satisfy their thirst for knowledge. Within such environment the child becomes not only the stream of knowledge but also the ocean of knowledge. While discussion with his friends the child expands the periphery of his experiences. He has number of ways to satisfy his hunger for knowledge. Nevertheless their first choice for satisfying hunger for knowledge is only the teacher. Alas! Many teachers of today are found lacking in this aspect. Consequently, the student who considered the teacher as the source of knowledge has started to doubt him. The student who believed the teacher's words to be the ultimate truth (Brahma) in yester years, now tests the teacher's truthfulness after going home or while being his friends. Why is it so? You have the knowledge of your own subject only; whereas the student has the knowledge of all subjects taught in his school and beyond that he has the knowledge of all subjects of his interest and aptitude. So who is more knowledgeable? Often it is heard in the classroom that mathematics teacher has inadequate knowledge of language, whereas the language teacher may not have adequate knowledge of science. Irrespective of the teacher's subject, the student is interested in how and how much he can impart it.

In such circumstances, it is the teacher's good fortune that the student possessing good knowledge in many subjects trusts the teachers with honour and respect. What would be the fate of the teacher if he is asked to take test of Talent search or Quiz competition? To-day's student is not satisfied with bookish knowledge only. Are we, as teachers, capable to give information required or sought by the students? To maintain status and respectability, the teacher must possess enough knowledge. He must see to it that he does not become an unwanted teacher. The teacher of to-day and tomorrow must resort to deep reading of educative and informative books, magazines etc. He must also view various informative and educational TV-channels to enrich and upgrade his knowledge and skills. He will have to resort to chatting and surfing also.

With a view to assessing the effectiveness of his teaching, he must undertake an action research. The outcome will enable him to improve classroom interaction and behaviour.

Let me exhort the teachers to be well-equipped and knowledgeable in this era of knowledge and technology with these words: Oh Teachers! Arise, awake and stop not till you achieve the latest knowledge and skills.

Note:

Teacher has the knowledge of his own subject only; whereas the student has the knowledge of all subjects taught in his school and beyond that he has the knowledge of all subjects of his interest and aptitude. So who is more knowledgeable?

9

LET THE CLASS ROOM TEACHER BE A COMMUNITY TEACHER

Aim of education is not limited to imparting literacy to a person. Education aims at the all-round development of the person and makes him live a better life with progress. It comprises acquisition of knowledge, psycho-physical development, character formation, emotional integrity, preservation and promotion of culture and national integration. It also purports to make the person free from narrow-mindedness and selfishness and thereby to make him social. The person who imparts education is popularly known as the teacher. It is more significant to become a real teacher in practice rather than being identified as a degree-holder. The persons who do not have a degree for teaching but are devoted to community welfare work are commonly known as LOKSHIKSHAK (community teacher). Let us remember a few such community teachers and salute them.

Thanks to many such community teachers, a number of persons have got inspiration for better living and achieving progress in life. Although the means and methods of educating the masses were different, their mission was to help the people achieve their progress as well as the development of the community. We recognise several community welfare workers as saints, social reformers, devotees or literary persons. In fact, for them, fame or title has no importance, but their deeds are very significant. Many social reformers like Dayanand Sarasvati, Gandhiji, Vinoba Bhave and Raja Rammohan Roy have helped many persons to improve themselves and tried to eradicate many social evils. Many devotees such as Narsinh Mehta, Mirabai, Jalaram Bapa, Ganga Sati and the like have tried their best in reforming the society. All of them have tried their best to help people turn towards devotion to God. Through their devotional literature, they created self-confidence in them and helped them become social and spiritual human beings.

Just think of their efforts! To create literature and propagate it themselves! In their times, the facilities as at present were not available. Despite this, they have worked so diligently and deeply that even the present generation is making use of their literature and reading material. We identify such community welfare workers who have significantly contributed to the arousal of the masses, only as literary persons. To cite a few of them, they are: Premanand, Akho, Narmad, Zaverchand Meghani, Dula Bhaya Kag and the like. They have created literature in the language of the people with a view to bringing about change in the individual as well as in the society, keeping in view the need of contemporary people and the society.

Today also there are many Lokshikshaks (Community welfare workers), thanks to them from whom quite a good number of people have obtained the way of living life, ability and inspiration for good life. They are Shri Pramukh Swami, Shri Morari Bapu, Shri Ramesh Oza and Shri Kiritbhaiji. Shri SaiRam Dave also has his own style as Lokshikshak. Shri Bhikhudan Gadhavi who has acquired less formal education has become Lokshikshak by doing socially useful work. He depends mainly on the literary contributions of Shri Zaverchand Meghani and Shri Dula Bhaya Kag. With sentiment of laughter, he points out the social evils to be eradicated, and sets the people thinking.

The society is bright thanks to the Lokshikshaks (community welfare workers), not due to the Degree-holder teachers. The presence or attendance in the formal classrooms is dwindling, whereas the Lokshikshak's audience is innumerable even during summer, or sometimes at night also. Son, daughter and the parents willingly attend Lokshikshak's night classes.

There is no guarantee that a trained graduate teacher will succeed as a teacher, whereas Lokshikshaks are self-made; formal education or a Degree has no great significance for them. Quite a few trained teachers find it a difficult job to teach and manage a class of fifty to sixty students; whereas the open air classes of a Lokshikshak have thousands of persons listening to him with rapt attention for not less than two hours. He has his own style of presentations of the theme; he can sing, he has his style of playing on instruments, and even resorts to acting also. He becomes successful because of these skills. The Lokshikshaks take their work as duty, whereas the Degree holder teacher looks at his work as mere service. Hence the Lokshikshaks are more respected than the traditional teachers.

Government on its own honours Lokshikshak with awards, whereas the traditional teacher has to apply for it with necessary certificates and credentials. Lokshikshaks are honoured, time and again by the society. For instance, Shri Bhikhudan Gadhvi, the Lokshikshak, having less formal education has been honoured with Gaurav Award from Gujarat government, Shri Ravishankar Maharaj Award and Delhi Academy of Music and Drama Award. Lokshikshak Dula Bhaya Kag with schooling up to Class Five had been awarded title 'Padmashri' from Government of India. Service to humanity for arousing social awareness, rendered by revered Shri Moraribapu, Shri Shahbuddin Rathod and Sai Ram Dave is commendable.

Note: *The persons who do not have a degree for teaching but are devoted to community welfare work are commonly known as community teacher.*

10

TEACHERS SHOULD EXAMINE THE ANSWER BOOKS DEVOTEDLY

The Gujarat Secondary School Examination Board holds examinations for Classes 10 and 12 every year. The students try their best to get the result as best as they can after having strenuously prepared for it. Even their parents (guardians) would not have cared even for their jobs or occupations to encourage their sons / daughters to come out with the best result. They must have spent a large amount of money, and they must have coveted many aspirations for them. Moreover, counseling centers are also opened by the Secondary Education Board in Gujarat State to help the candidates overcome any type of difficulty or fear regarding the examination.

All efforts by the school authority as well as by the Government to see that the examinees get good result by taking examination in good atmosphere have been welcomed by the students as well as the guardians. They have given full co-operation too. The students have tried their level best to note down their answers in answer-books within the stipulated time duration of three hours. They have thus fulfilled their responsibility and reposed on the evaluators. Then starts the extremely important duty of teachers! The evaluating teachers should try their best to do justice to the examinees through the qualitative aspect of their answer books as per merit.

The Gujarat Secondary School Board has been showing the examined answer-books of the Class-12 students on payment of the necessary fees by the guardians, personally to the student (examinee) concerned and his guardian, for their satisfaction. In the past, cases have been reported where teachers (examiners) were found not to have evaluated answer books properly. In such cases, the marks given by the examiner were less than what the examinee (student) deserved for the answer. Not only that, in several cases, it was strange to see that the examiner had crossed the answer with red-ink pen, even if the student's answer was correct and his all the labour is lost in red ink. In such cases, even if the guardian lodges a complaint, it proves futile. The reason is that the assessment (or marks) by the examining teacher is final as per rule in such cases.

In examinations of Classes 10 and 12 of General Stream, the answer books are not shown in person. Is it possible that such cases do not occur even in those examinations? It is so because of the administrative problems and reasons. It is accepted that sometimes while examining the answer books error is committed. Even then it is never acceptable when the student (examinee) becomes the victim of the teacher's (examiner's) error. In majority of such cases, such improper evaluation is done not due to the examiner's error, but simply because of his negligence. One or two such undesirable actions can be considered mistakes or errors, but such frequently occurring instances can be ascribed to sheer negligence or intention.

The examiners alone can be considered responsible for the improper evaluation of the answer-books. What can the Secondary Education Board or the Government do in such cases? The reason is: In order that the answer-books are examined very qualitatively, the examiners are required to assess only twenty answer books of Class 12 students of Science stream. Here the answer books are to be examined, not to be observed. It is the practice that the same answer book is scrutinized by more than one examiner. Hence it is the full responsibility of only the examiners to see that the answer books are evaluated properly and qualitatively. Hence the examiners alone can be considered responsible for improper evaluation.

Wherever the Board requires the examiner to go for assessing the answer books, he should go there and assess the answer books with full sincerity. He should consider such work as his important duty. The process of assessing the answer books is a psycho-emotive work. Hence the examiner should bear in mind certain important aspects while assessing the answer books of the candidates. The writer addresses the teachers and offers some 'do's and don'ts' regarding the assessment of the answer books. You expect sincerity of assessment of your son's / daughter's answer books. Assess the answer books of all other candidates with the same spirit and sincerity. Don't be liberal or stern while assessing the answer boooks but be a votary of excellence. Read with enough consciousness what the candidate has written and assign marks with the same awareness. Take adequate care to see that no injustice is done to the good writing and also that the weak writing does not get undue benefit.

Follow the key for evaluation, but if it is needed, also insist on correct evaluation, understanding the examinee's originality. Avoid misbeliefs. For instance, eighty marks in Gujarati subject should not be and cannot be given at all. Assign adequate period of time to assess each answer-book. Do not insist on assessing a fixed number of answer-books in a definite period of time. Make friendship with those teachers whose answer-paper-assessment is just and correct. Try to adopt that approach. Let not the inconvenience of the assessment-centre affect your assessment work. Apart from your likes and dislikes, if you work with enough sincerity as a teacher, every examinee assigned to you will get due justice. The teacher who brightens the student's future is the real teacher. Try to fulfil your responsibility of assessing the answer-books with care and diligence and do justice to the student's work.

Note:

- *The process of assessing the answer books is a psycho-emotive work.*

11

STRONG REASONS FOR BECOMING A TEACHER

*I*t is a common impression for teacher's profession that one who fails to get a job anywhere enters upon the teaching profession. This statement or belief is not true at present. In the present context, however, quite a good number of persons have accepted teaching as a profession. Despite this, there are many who are against accepting teacher's job. Here we shall discuss about why the teacher's profession should be accepted and what benefit does the person get by becoming a teacher.

Teacher's profession is considered pious compared to other occupations. He (the teacher) has a definite position in the society and enjoys unique status in the society; and that is unparalleled. Any other person occupying the high-ranking position in other occupations would always address him as "Sir" with respect, even if he is the owner or the manager of a company, the Judge of the court, the District Superintendent of Police or even the Collector of the district. This itself dignifies the teaching profession; and it is conspicuous by its absence in other occupations. Even the villagers bow down and pay respect to the teacher when he passes by.

Thus the teacher is respected by the society at large. He has job satisfaction. He sees and knows the result of his work so soon, which always enhances his self-confidence. If the boy/girl does not perform well or does not pass at the examination, it is largely he or she who is blamed, not the teacher. Such a positive attitude for the teacher has no parallel in other occupations.

When the teacher is teaching in the classroom, the students usually listen to him with respect. Generally, they never distrust him. Teaching is the only profession in which the teacher can shape their minds according to his philosophy and thinking easily. Thus as a teacher he can prepare and mould a large class according to his ideology. He enjoys working with living persons and gets job satisfaction. Sometimes he has to face a challenge, which makes his work more lively.

As regards the period of work, the teacher is required to go to the school in time. No extra time for duty before or after school timings is required to be assigned to him, as is done for office work in other occupations. The quantum of work done in other occupations is either judged or noted at the end of the day's work, whereas in the case of teaching, no such daily note is required about how and how much teaching is done daily. In teaching profession the salaries of the teachers are adequate for maintenance of life.

For additional income the teacher takes up tuitions of students, even though the government does not approve it. The guardians are pleased or willing to approach teachers for the tuition of their sons or daughters. Thus he has no worry about the maintenance of life. If he is a teacher in a non-government school or a college he is not liable to be transferred to a remote place.

Moreover, the teacher has enough opportunities to undertake leadership in society during various social events or national celebrations. He can spend enough time for amusement, trips, excursions with family to religious places or places of historical importance. He can spend times freely with his family after school hours of work. In the institutions of higher education, he may report late, finish his assigned work and leave the institution earlier with prior intimation and freely attend to other engagements.

A teacher is required to teach the students the subject of his interest, namely, language, science, mathematics, social studies, as assigned by the Principal. He does not feel workload or any tension about whether he can do it or not. On the other hand, he is free to adopt innovative approach to the teaching of the assigned subject. Thus by adopting different methods of teaching, he can bring diversity in teaching new units of the subjects. The freedom of handling the work in the way and to the degree he likes is given to him as the teacher. He is, so to say, the king of the classroom.

His students in future might have been working in various fields. For instance, some may become doctors (physicians), some may be engineers, some others may join civil services, may be even in clerical jobs, police officers or in postal services or railways. It is but natural that all of them may be helpful, when necessary. Where great officers might be finding it difficult to get the work done, the teacher gets it done easily. It is so because in every field of work, he finds some one or the other of his past students working there. It is rarely found to have similar situation in other occupations.

Note:

- Teacher's profession is considered pious compared to other occupations.
- *The teacher has enough opportunities to undertake leadership in society during various social events or national celebrations.*

12

A TEACHER IS ALSO A GUARDIAN

A few days back I happened to meet a teacher couple. During discussion on education, child behaviour and child education were also referred to. On the basis of their talk, I felt that they were not fully satisfied with the nature of their child's education, and that they were keeping that matter secret from me. However I clearly asked them: Are you content with your child's education? With hesitation, they agreed: "We feel that our child has not developed to the extent of his latent potential. The couple left my company after about an hour long meeting with me. But, thereafter, a number of thoughts occupied my mind. I started visualizing the children of the teachers of my acquaintance and recalled their parents. I felt that quite a good number of parents did not spare time for their children's education to the extent that was needed. I have used the phrase: 'did not spare' ... instead of 'could not spare'. The readers of this article should, specially, take note of this.

I just lightly initiated this discussion in the staff room of my college. With reservation I declared that the children of around fifty per cent of the teachers are usually not outstanding in either learning or co-curricular activities, so to say, they are only mediocre. The teacher sitting next to me ventured to correct my estimate and declared not fifty but around eighty per cent teachers' children may be ordinary in studies. However, it is a fact that the advice they give to the guardians for their children to improve their performance, is not followed by themselves in regard to their own children. I would venture to remark: "Do you spare that much period of time for your children's study to improve their standard or their level of excellence, as you do in the case of others?" The answer is: With regrets, no! Mad after tuitions to increase bank balance, the teacher later on is found running madly to seek admission for his son or daughter in institutions for higher studies, of course, with preparation to pay even donation! But alas! He fails to secure admission for his son or daughter in a good or reputed institution of higher education. Instead of collecting money through tuitions to help improve the level of learning of others' children, the tutor should take care to see that the present and the future of his children is not spoiled.

At present, quite a good number of teachers are found giving more importance to the school than to their home. They attach more importance to their students rather than to their own children. Perhaps this reflects the teacher's feelings and sincerity! Even then, it is so much important for him to spare adequate period of time for his family including the learning children. In this regard, the sincere teachers should prepare a specific plan for their period of time and the schedule of their work. Failing which, when they return home late after school hours and the tuition schedule, they find often their children asleep! How can such father help his child secure all-round development? The tragedy of the fact is that such teachers happen to advise the parents or guardians to take care of their children's learning and education as such!

Lady teachers have different problems. In the man-dominated society, she has either to attend to kitchen work or other domestic work. That is why they may not or cannot attend to the child's care or education adequately. They must devote more time for the child's education or study in preference to her domestic work. Such care and treatment for the child's development and education by her would bring out positive result in favour of the child.

At present, several teachers are found to have joined in some sort of community service. The community seems to have more trust in their ability and ingenuity. Nevertheless they must take care that they do not harm the well-being of the family, while trying to improve the community. In time to come it would be your own members of the family and your offspring to help you in future. Nature and care or culture given to them by you will be reflected on you in your future life. Let me ask: How many teachers devote two to three hours with their children? How many teachers have told stories or taken them to visit places of interest to them like zoo or picnic spots or places of historical interest? How many teachers accept the request of the child to take him for a walk and have some light refreshment?

Several teachers do agree that the potential capabilities of the child must be developed. We should expect the performance of the child only according to his abilities. As you sow, so you reap. This proverb holds well in regard to the care and nurturing of the child.

On the other side, there is a limited group of a few teachers, who are sincere and duty conscious not only to the school but to their families, especially to their developing sons and daughters also. Such teachers provide an exemplary model for the rest of the teacher fraternity in regard to the care and development of their children on right lines. With these words, I conclude: Be a good and responsible teacher as well as an affectionate guardian.

Note:

- *We should expect the performance of the child only according to his abilities.*

13

LET US ASSIGN ONE MINUTE MORE FOR STUDENTS

*L*et me cite a real incident that occurred in USA (United States of America). A person started a grocery store. After two years, he had in all eleven stores in operation with full swing (vigorously). Someone questioned him, "How is it that you could start ten other new stores within a short span of two years only? Over and above, every store operates extremely well. The customers do not go to other stores for purchase so long as your store is open. The store owner's reply was: we allot one minute every week for each customer. The person who was inquiring could not understand what the owner meant to say. The store owner explained saying, "We keep the stores closed on every Saturday and Sunday. Every Friday before leaving I sit with all employees for one minute for each. During the meeting we discuss about what innovative features for the customers we should introduce next week so that they feel more satisfied. All of us discuss and decide just one point: What novelty should we introduce next week? In this way, we decide one new point every week. In accordance with the agreed new point, we make necessary changes in our behaviour or method of working or arrangements of things.

Thus our stores introduce something new for the customers every week. Consequently the customers gradually feel more satisfied and we get enthusiasm. Our customers are pleased, hence we are also pleased.

Let us think of a parallel situation in the field of education. In the school or college, the staff (teaching as well as non-teaching) may get together with one minute agenda. Every member may present a point regarding something new to do. Out of several innovative ideas or approaches thus suggested, let them agree on one such point. Let that new approach or thing be put into action during the second week. As soon as the second week is over, once again one minute agenda is to be taken up! New point may be decided and executed accordingly. Considering this way, in school or college, minimum a period of forty weeks (after deducting vacation periods) may be available for forty innovative ideas to be implemented. Thus the teachers and the students would be found busy doing something or the other new or in a new way every time all the year round. All of them may get inspiration from one another and work with delight. Then the overall result is bound indeed to be good.

In such matters the Principal of the institution or one of the Trustees may take the leadership. If nobody is prepared to accept such responsibility, or no other person is prepared for such thinking, the teacher on his own may implement such innovative idea. The teacher, on his own, may decide what novelty he would introduce the next week so that the students may get more satisfaction and joy. Keep up the new adopted during the past week, while introducing any other novel feature for the next week. Whatever new idea or feature accepted during the previous week is also to be kept up, even when another novelty is introduced for the next week. The nature of the novelty or innovation depends upon the human as well as the physical factors. Certain matters or approaches can be easily accepted and put into practice. For instance, the members of the teaching as well as non-teaching staff may decide to talk or behave with others with a smile on their faces, to speak with or call each other with full respects, even if he is a student. The teacher can introduce some new technique or elements during classroom transaction. It is necessary to think first and then act accordingly.

There are other advantages also of putting the above-mentioned idea of innovation into action. If you think about new order, it will be done. The absence of new thinking reduces the possibility of new order to occur at all. Some time situational factors hinder the execution of the new order. You should not be disappointed in such situation. Group thinking and consideration is necessary, prior to the commencement of any work or project. Group decision-making enhances the index of success. The institutional physical as well as emotional environment changes positively. All employees (teaching as well as non teaching) would sincerely co-operate with the spirit of fraternity in the execution of the new order. They would own the responsibility of low result or failure. The very change in their minds is a positive sign to lead the institution on the path of development and progress. New thinking brings out new things. Monotonous work every day becomes tiresome. Stagnant water causes foul smell. Thus in the same way when no change takes place in the institute, it may turn dormant. One, who keeps on introducing new dimensions in his work, will remain in place for long; otherwise he will be thrown away. This applies to the teacher also. Can a person without honour and status be a teacher?

If the institution or the teacher puts this idea in to practice, the students will be attracted towards that institution or the teacher concerned. The guardians will also take note of such good work and appreciate it. Other schools or teachers will also take note of it. The result is quite evident that the status of the teachers as well as of the institution will be elevated. The teachers will also develop self-confidence. You cannot think how much benefitted are the students by your allotment of one minute for novel idea or action. If the teachers begin to think in this way to introduce novel features in their work, the non teaching members of the staff will also begin to think positively in the same way. This situation will, indeed have a positive impact on students as well as the guardians/parents: change in clothing, change in food, change in socks and foot wear. Let me say: man cannot live without change. 'Nothing is permanent, only change is permanent.' Hence the problem is: How could the teacher live without change? Even today there may be several teachers whose quality and quantity of thinking seem to be the same as they were when they joined the service! Their style of teaching also remains unchanged. Hence, as the change enhances joy for life (and living), the change in technique and method of teaching would also contribute to enhancing joy and satisfaction of the teacher and the learners also.

The author saw such new approach being adopted recently in two secondary schools. Let it serve as an inspiration for other schools. One such school is D.P. High school situated

Dr. Ashok Patel

in New Vadaj of Ahmadabad city in India, being managed
by Shri Jaydev Sonagara. The Principal holds a meeting with
the teachers for one hour every Saturday, during which the
work done during the week is assessed and the planning for
the next week is done regularly. The record of the minutes
of the meeting is always maintained. Henceforth all the
members of the teaching staff have resolved to add some
novel feature every week. The other school is Shri Swami-
Narayan High School, Ranip (Ahmedabad city area). In this
School, the students evaluate the teacher's every period of
teaching. The student who is assigned to prepare a written
summary of the observation prepares a brief report about
what the teacher concerned did during the period and how
he did so etc. The brief report is handed over to the Trustee
concerned every day for perusal. If needed, suggestions or
inspiration is provided to the teacher concerned. In the
school concerned, every teacher is observed to be very active
during each period of teaching. Here the more pleasing
aspect was that the students were neutral in evaluation.

Note:

- *Group decision-making enhances the index of success.*
- *Nothing is permanent, only change is permanent.*

14

SKILL IS MORE IMPORTANT THAN KNOWLEDGE

*A*ctivity is an important medium to impart and to acquire education. Aims of education, in order, are: acquisition of knowledge, understanding, application and development of skills. An individual, first of all, acquires knowledge. Knowledge does not mean only information. The information may be useful in only answering questions. In life, knowledge is more important than information. It is more important to have comprehension of knowledge than simply information. Hence the comprehension of the acquired knowledge is the second aim of education. The proper application (use) of the acquired knowledge and understanding in living (life) can be considered the third aim of education. The last and the most important aim of education is the acquisition of skills. The education imparted in the classroom or outside the school or college is said to be significant only when the student acquires the skills of his interest. That is why Gandhiji had considered 'Craft' learning as the compulsory skill-acquisition and development in school education.

In the present day school learning, craft-learning has no place; or say, it has been exiled. Nevertheless, some schools, considering it their moral as well as important duty, have been organizing several activities with a view to developing various skills in students. The society should publicly honour such schools. Government tries to some extent to encourage schools as well as colleges busy with activities, the response to which is very poor. Interschool or inter-collages competitions are also organised by some social groups or government, keeping some specific skills in view, which may be in students' interests. When the inter-schools or inter-colleges activities are organised, (then) only those students well-versed in that particular skill can take advantage and encouragement thereof. With a view to helping every student to develop some particular skills, every school or college should organise activities on its own campus, on its own way, keeping the students in view. Thus maximum number of students can participate and develop specific skills.

In our opinion, those schools or colleges are the best institutions that have such planning as would help all students to develop skills of their interest by participating in the activities concerned. Some schools or colleges, though deemed small, have excellent performance in this regard. The Vidyanagar High School situated in Usmanpura (Ahmedabad) is very famous for the last so many years for celebrating festivals of aesthetic aspects as well as games and sports. Moreover the newly started schools may also create confidence and trust among children and their parents / guardians through such planning.

The writer had an occasion to visit I.D. Patel School campus in Ghatlodiya (Ahmedabad) area. He was very much pleased to see the work done by them. There was not a single pupil who would have lost an opportunity of developing his skills. The effective communication between the teachers and the taught was a positive indication that the future of India is bright. Along with cultural programmes, various games, Yoga-Asanas, drum and Lezim, various exercises and an exhibition of hundreds of educational and value-based items prepared with the students' active participation- were exhibited effectively. Presentation by young children through computer, book exhibition, also the presentation in English by the children with Gujarati as mother tongue: the educationists and the guardians were astonished with the entire presentation. How delightful it would be if other schools also try to emulate this model!

If it so happens, various skills will be developed in children. In addition, the virtues like group spirit, family feeling, discipline, planning, responsibility and leadership would also begin to develop. These, in future, would be beneficial to the society as well as to the country. It was also observed that the small schools used to encourage their students to pay visit to such excellent school as encouragement to them. It is a matter of joy that the students of other schools augmented their knowledge by visiting that renowned school. On the other hand, the problem of the development of skills of the students of other schools remains unanswered. Unless and until the adequate development of some specific skills in an individual is not achieved, it cannot be said that he has achieved all-round development. The function of the school as well as the college is not simply to impart knowledge to the students but to help them develop certain specific skills also.

Instead of giving importance to the bookish knowledge, the schools and colleges are expected to shoulder the responsibility of imparting skill-oriented training to the students. This may be naturally expected by the citizens at large. A good teacher is he who prefers to teach by doing rather than talking. He is the best teacher who involves the students into doing some relevant action or skillful activity for learning.

Note: The function of the school as well as the college is not simply to impart knowledge to the students but to help them develop certain specific skills also.

15

DEVOTION IS MORE IMPORTANT THAN RULE

*F*ormal Education comprises classroom instruction (teaching), co-curricular activities, school management, teacher-parent relationship and so on. I feel perhaps research on the relationship between the effective development of these aspects and the qualitative outcome vis-a-vis rules and human sincerity may be undertaken. Here I would like to restrict my discussion only to the school management (school organisation and administration).

I had many occasions to visit a number of schools for educational purpose. This schedule has become a sort of routine. During the visit, I have discussions with the Principal, the teachers and sometimes with even the students. This helps me to know about the emotional environment of the school. The development of an institution depends upon the strength of its emotional environment. But how can such a healthy emotional environment be built up? Here are the ways to secure it:

- Every one concerned including teachers must come to the school regularly in time.

- The teacher should teach the subject matter with student's active participation in the teaching - learning process.
- Any decision of yours should be in the interest of the institution.
- Everybody in the institution should perform his duty with a sense of fraternity and be helpful to others whenever needed.
- Love the learner in the school as you love your child.
- Try to encourage students in co-curricular activities.

Can such wishful thinking bring any positive change in the mental set-up of the teaching and non-teaching staff of the school?

I have visited many educational institutions. My impression is that the institution that gives more importance to sincerity and dedication possesses the entire personnel, from peon to Principal, working with devotion in the interest of students and the institution. How good it would be if the Principal inquires about the health of the teacher, when he reports late for duty, in stead of scolding him? Can not the Principal arrange for light refreshment for the teacher when he is overburdened with work? How good it would be about the staff members if they extend monetary help to the peons on good as well as untoward situations! What a good gesture it would be on the part of the Principal if he goes out of his way and makes alternative arrangement in case of the teacher feeling unwell or uncomfortable when on duty in school ? Such humanitarian attitude and treatment help positively in building up socio-emotional environment in the school.

Problems of maintaining discipline are bound to arise till the socio-emotional environment is not created in the institution. It is the first and the foremost responsibility of the management as well as the head of the institution to build up and help maintain healthy, emotional and social environment in the institution. If they try to understand the mentality and the problems of the employees, (then) the employees would, indeed, respond positively. Showing rules and provisions on either side would never end the problem till the humanitarian approach is adopted. Sincerity, devotion and dedication on both the sides would help strengthen the socio-emotional and humane environment of the institution. Thus love and affection along with mutual understanding goes a long way in maintaining healthy environment in the school. A person can be won through love, and not fear.

For the development of an institution, every employee should discharge his duty diligently and sincerely; and thus help promote the emotional and social environment of the institution. The Head of the institution has a vital role to play in this regard.

Note:

- Teacher has to love the learner in the school as he loves his child.
- The development of an institution depends upon the strength of its emotional environment.

16

A TEACHER HAS TO MOULD THE CHILD

A teacher is such a job-oriented person from whom the maximum numbers of persons have maximum expectations. That is why purity and devotion are connected with this profession. In case some doctor, pleader, conductor or a person from any other vocation misbehaves, the society may somewhat criticise it and then forgets it. But if the similar misbehavior is done by a teacher, the society would harass him. It becomes troublesome to come out of his residence. This matter itself proves that the society has specific expectations in great measure and in every way. It is, therefore, the teacher's moral as well as major/comprehensive duty to fulfil that expectation. No teacher can afford to be deficient in such matter.

Every child sees the teacher in status higher than even God. After having reached the youth, he may perhaps feel shy to touch the parent's feet (in reverence), nor would he bow down. But when the teacher comes in front of him in the bazaar, even at noon, he would neither hesitate nor feel ashamed to bow down and pay respects to the teacher. Even the parents/guardians show respect for the teacher. If any teacher goes to the guardian's shop or office, his behaviour with him (the guardian) would be full of respect. All teachers should try their best to maintain the guardians' such trust for them. Every guardian sends his child/ward to the teacher with trust and great expectation; not only to learn or study (not for literacy alone). If this much had been the expectation, even the guardian could fulfill it with one hour's daily effort at home. The teacher's name only while scolding the misbehaving child is enough to stop him to misbehave. That is the proof of the teacher's influence even when he is physically absent. The teacher has to sustain this influence.

As the potter gives shape to an earthen pot, so has the teacher to mould a child. Just recall the potter giving shape to an earthen pot from a lump of wet clay. What different types of processes does he use on the lump of wet clay so as to shape it in the form of a durable and quality earthen pot? The lumps of wet clay used to shape them into pots are different. Some may contain small pebbles or some may have useless material in them. Same may be wet or some may have less water. The potter applies various processes and takes more or less period of time in turning the wheel with concentration of mind. Thus he finally gives good and desired shape to the pot on wheel.

As the speciality of each lump of mud is different, so the children also have varied specialities. Some may be strong; or some others may be weak. Some may be more intelligent, while some others may possess less intelligence. Some children learn rapidly, while some are slow learners. Some remember for a long period of time, whereas some may forget quickly. Some child may rarely fall ill, whereas some may remain in constant sickness. The teacher should identify the factors that intervene the child's learning, try to remove them and shape him well. As the potter fulfils his aim with patience and confidence, the teacher should also trust the child, work with patience and has to help in his development.

Here we should not forget the fact that the potter has to work with inanimate things, whereas the teacher has to work with living individuals. Hence the teacher's job assumes greater importance and becomes very difficult also. So the society respects the teacher; the students as well as the guardians/parents bow down to him. Take for example a hypothetical case of a doctor or a pleader. Ask him to satisfy the needs of around fifty persons sitting before him, at a time. It is simply impossible. The teacher has to do such a difficult task. If he does his job sincerely very well and in a gratifying manner, he will be duly respected, If his approach and style of fulfilling his task is unique, he will indeed be publicly honored too.

Note:

- *Every child sees the teacher in status higher than even God.*
- *Arising of questions is a sign of progress.*

17

A TEACHER SHOULD BE A CONSTANT LEARNER

Stagnant water gives out foul smell – according to this saying, a person also should try to keep on flowing. This flow means the act of running to achieve the goal. Besides, the teacher on whom the society has unique trust and on whom the new generation depends has to help the children develop along with his own development. In view of this, how could he afford to be in a standstill position? The teacher should, therefore, keep himself constantly learning; and for that he should go on improving himself.

There is no age limit for learning. An acquaintance of the writer (of this article) had acquired LL.M. degree at the age of 67 years. He did so not for any vocation, but for self-joy only. With a view to achieving skill or proficiency in the vocation that you are engaged, you have got to learn continuously. You have to do so also to enable you to perform your duty as best as you can. In the classroom, the teacher is used teaching any one subject, whereas the students would be learning more than one subject. In that case if any teacher says that he has the knowledge of only his subject that will not do. The reason is that he should correlate the subject-matter with other subject while teaching his subject. Through such correlation, the students can understand the subject-matter easily; and they are also delighted to learn. Because of the development of science and technology, educational tools and instruments have also changed. Hence the teacher should collect the necessary information about such appliances and also learn how to use them. In this way, he will be able to teach his subject with ease and interest.

It should be worth remembering that a person learns less from others, but he learns more by himself. Anything taught by others may be forgotten quickly, but what is learned personally will be remembered for long. Every teacher should remember again and again the statement: "I am learning while teaching. I have, more likely, forgotten what others have taught me, I remember only that which I have learned myself." Thus, inspired from his own work, the teacher should continue learning himself.

The teacher has to lead the students to the new world. Hence he himself has to acquire the new world's knowledge and experience. For this, more reading and more use of technology would be helpful. He should remain fully informed continuously through the use of TV, computer and internet. Then only he will be able to impart something new to the students. If the teacher claims that he knows everything or that he is well-versed in his subject, then that teacher is wrong. Every teacher should remember that his knowledge is limited to only his subject, whereas his students have the knowledge of many subjects. Today the students entering the classroom possess so much information and other things that the teacher's information falls much short compared to that as such. At times what the teacher brings by way of information would be found stale for the students.

The teacher usually instructs the students to make regular efforts daily for two-three hours in study at home. In this context the teacher also should make more efforts in updating his knowledge before teaching the subject. Only then he can surpass the students in knowledge. The present-day student does not like yesterday's stale information. He wants everything fresh or quite new every day. To satisfy or fulfil this need of the students, the teacher has to learn ceaselessly the new vistas of education.

The present-day generation of students is more interested in observing and doing than listening. A person can learn better by observing than hearing. The teacher has therefore to bring change in the technique of classroom teaching. It is necessary for the teacher to make the students the observers rather than the listeners. He is the best teacher who makes the students 'learn by doing.' If the information given in the text-book only is necessary to be imparted to the students in the classroom, the student can do it on his own at home. Besides imparting information, the teacher should also make him skilful. He has to make him a thoughtful person as well. If no questions arise in the students' mind after the teacher's teaching, it means that the teacher has either not taught him well or the student has not rightly understood it. Arising of questions is a sign of progress. Arising of critical and logical questions in student's mind is necessary. And the teacher must be capable to answer them.

In many schools, quite a good number of teachers are found constantly diligent. They are learning new aspects of teaching or education. Inspired from them, other teachers also are found trying to learn something new, whereas some teachers believe in maintaining status quo. Let us expect such teachers to make transformation as early as possible in themselves as well as in their ideology and become a source of inspiration for other teachers.

Note:

- *Anything taught by others may be forgotten quickly, but what is learned personally will be remembered for long.*
- *He is the best teacher who makes the students 'learn by doing.'*

18

WANTED POETRY TEACHERS

*N*owadays the educationists or the linguists are not at all satisfied with the teaching of language in schools or colleges. The teachers have altogether changed the purpose itself of language teaching. The main objectives of teaching a language are to develop the four main skills: listening, speaking, reading and writing; moreover to help the students to take interest in literature, in addition, to impart the knowledge of grammar. It is felt that the teachers rarely teach grammar. It is not an exaggeration at all in saying that the poetry teaching has become defunct. Here the writer wants to discuss the important aspects of poetry teaching. Poetry is, so to say, the subject to be experienced; it cannot be taught or learnt like a prose; it is to be enjoyed, or experienced emotionally.

During classroom teaching, the majority of teachers turns the poetry into prose and then explains the meaning. Had the poet meant to convey only the meaning, why should he have taken the great effort to compose the poetry? It would have served the purpose, if he had written down a passage of prose.

Some teachers, while teaching a poem, paraphrase it into explaining difficult words, figure of speech, verse, compound and so on, as if they are explaining grammar to the students. Thus they destroy the charm of the poem itself. The poem consists of emotion, union and ascent more than a prose. When the poem is sung with music, the emotional flow develops in full swing. The elements strengthening body, mind and soul develop fully when the poetry is turned into the musical song. The poet has, therefore, composed the poetry. The poetry is not to be learnt but to be experienced; it is to be enjoyed. We have to become co-partners of the poet's emotions. The teacher has to help the learners enjoy the world of imagination beyond knowledge. The teacher has to develop the essence of the poetry in such a way that the student is dragged into its stream of essence. During such experience, he would enjoy the beauty of the poem. The teacher has to refrain from explaining its meaning. Thus the poem / poetry is not to be taught but to be caught. Let the students enjoy the world of imagination. Do not try to impede their ability of imagination.

During poetry teaching, try to draw the students' attention towards how the poet has expressed his emotions rather than what he has told. Let them enjoy learning poetry. The fact that they have enjoyed could be judged from the emotional expressions on their faces. Even some of them might be found murmuring or reciting a few lines of the poetry! The poetry should not be presented through only words. It must be sung and enjoyed with emotive expression.

Out of the four Vedas, the Samaved is so prepared that it can be sung. The Vedic verses of the Samaved can be sung. In Samaved around 1875 verses have been composed which are addressed to Fire, Indra Somrasa and others. The style of presentation of so many verses is so impressive that it is exciting. Many other ancient treatises have been composed in the form of metrical compositions, which must have been a strenuous job of those who might have composed them. When one thinks in this way, while teaching a poetry, the whole purpose will be altered. You know that maths is a difficult subject but the maths teacher enjoys teaching it. In this way poetry teaching may be difficult but the joy of teaching it must be felt in the class room.

The teacher who cannot enjoy the poetry himself cannot inspire the students to enjoy the same at all. On the contrary, it becomes a boring task, with the result that the students avoid leaning a poetry. In contrast, they are found enjoying and singing film songs, because they are presented with music. If the teacher recites the poetry with proper intonation or if he sings the poetry with rhythm, the students would join him and enjoy learning it. In fact, this is the essence of teaching and learning poetry. In future there would be the advertisement 'Poet teacher is required,' hence don't get surprised because all the language teachers are not the 'poet teachers.'

Note:

- *The poem is not to be taught but to be caught.*
- *The teacher who cannot enjoy the poetry himself cannot inspire the students to enjoy the same at all.*

19

CAN THE RETIRED TEACHER BECOME UNPRECEDENTED TEACHERS?

[The writer refers to his participation in a congregation of the former teachers of a school and his impressions]

It was an incident of a congregation of the former teachers of a school. The purpose was: to associate and stay with one another for the whole day, to deliberate, to exchange news about one another and enjoy the meeting with one another. It so happened that an idea sprang in a former teacher's mind: 'Let us get together and exchange views and news.' Another teacher responded positively, and encouraged him. As a result, on that day 23 former teachers of that school assembled together at 'the Environmental Sanitation Institute' situated on Ahmedabad – Gandhinagar Highway. Prior to this, every teacher came to school and from there only, they proceeded to the Institute concerned.

Gathering together in the school helped them to refresh their memories of the past experiences in the school. It was a pleasant experience for each one of them to share his pleasure with others. In the Environmental Sanitation

Institute, they stayed together for the whole day, took meals, held discussions, and became light-hearted and refreshed. They exchanged their present experiences and activities as the past teachers in the respective organisation at present. They conveyed their congratulations for the social work, to the respective organizations. They departed with the resolve to meet very often in time to come. Such incidents prove very beneficial to the persons concerned. They get joy and warmth as well as inspiration for good life in future.

Several ideas sprang up in the writer's mind as a result of his participation in the former teachers' congregation. Two matters are connected with the service in an institution. They are: Inactivity and devotion, Inactivity gives rise to slander, whereas joy in oneself is the result of devotion. Inactivity makes the person lifeless (useless), but devotion makes him producer. Many persons are not satisfied even during the period of retirement. Then the problem is: What have they done during the period of service? They are where they were if they do not feel satisfied at the end of that work. Two opinions are generally heard about how to spend time after retirement. Some friends say : "We want to take only rest, we have done much work". While several other friends say: "We want to remain active by engaging ourselves in some other activity of our choice." In true sense such an activity itself helps the man enjoy life, only rest harms him. When is the life of a person considered to be significant? It is said to be significant only to the extent to which he has worked for the welfare of the society, and not on the basis of how much he has done for himself during life. It is then only that the man can be considered social being in the true sense of the term. He cannot become a social person simply by living in society. We identify several persons living in society as antisocial persons. An idle and purposeless person is very dangerous for the society. Can we call them as antisocial or non-social persons? The present teacher or the past teacher is not only a social being, but he is the breath of society also. The breath of the society changes not only through his behaviour alone but through his words also. That is why Chanakya, the well-known economist of ancient time had said, "The teacher can never be ordinary".

Even after retirement some teachers cannot be free from the fascination for money. Such a wrong fascination for money itself damages his image as well as personality. After retirement some teachers are engaged in a variety of activities: proper or improper. For example, to join in some other occupation, to work as an agent for sale and purchase of land or building, to sit at the village 'Chora' or at crossing of four roads or society and indulge in criticising others. A few of the retired teachers would join themselves with social welfare institutions, undertake constructive activities in a village or society, or even read good literature. Out of these activities, those who undertake constructive work can be said to have turned their retirement period into socially useful work. For transforming the period of retirement into activity, a group of former teachers may be very useful. Such a group may consist of retired teachers of one school or of more than one school with an aim of undertaking social welfare activities. Many teachers have got retired. In short, as there is the association of the teachers, there should be also the association of the retired teachers and it would be more beneficial to the society at large. Perhaps such association may work more constructively and that too without selfish motives and thereby the government and the society would accept them very well.

Some past students who have been doing good work may also be visited by the former teachers, and they may discuss with them about the problems regarding the field of education. Consequently they may inform the authority concerned for future action. Some efficient former teachers may provide consulting services for the school that need them or that have poor results. Occasional visits by the former teachers to the hospital, orphanage and the house of the old forsaken parents may be sympathetic for them.

There are certain activates for the retired ones for their contribution to prove their sociability to visit the office of the past student working nicely, discuss educational problems and happening, and thereby the outcome of the discussions should be informed to the concerned person, institute or to the government, and if needed, the suggestions should be sent and take the government to task. And yes, for the outstanding performance encouragement must stand in need and to adopt a school and be a councillor. Even if the person is not a teacher, he can extend his service by joining hands with N G Os and doing social tasks at State, national or universal level. Any activities for educational reformation being undertaken by individual, institute or the government should be incorporated. Educational projects can be carried out by visiting the poor schools which have below 20% results; and benefit the students of such schools by your knowledge and experience. Thus a retired teacher can be a wonder teacher by being active in society at large.

Note:

- *The present teacher or the past teacher is not only a social being, but he is the breath of society also.*
- *A retired teacher can be a wonder teacher by being active in society at large.*

20

A TEACHER'S RETIREMENT MEANS AN END OF A PHILOSOPHY

*E*very government employee usually retires from service on completion of a stipulated age period. Even then the day of the teacher's retirement becomes a special day. The reason is: a teacher's retirement means so to say an end of a philosophy. Every teacher has a distinct personality. Likewise a difference is observed in his beliefs, insistence and principles also. In general, the students are thereby influenced to some extent. That is why it can be said that a teacher's retirement means an end of a philosophy. Besides this, thinking the other way, the teacher's retirement day becomes a special day, in which a special type of planning is made. This planning itself renders the teachers retirement distinct from the other programme of retirement.

It was specifically noted that the schools and colleges managed by good Trusts look distinct from other institutions. The family type of environment, corruption-free conduct, the activities of the institution as well as the financial assistance to the students – all these drew special attention. It is pleasurable to all to pay a visit to such institution. The teachers who were retiring also gave donation for the welfare of students. The activities of the social service committee are worth adopting, which is a distinguishing committee of the Vidyanagar High School, situated in Usmanpura (Ahmedaabd). The school offers financial assistance to the needy students, irrespective of students belonging to any school of any area of the city. One lakh rupees received by the then Principal Mr. Himmatbhai Kapasi at the time of retirement from that school were donated to the students of the same school for welfare activities. This serves as a good example worth emulating by schools for rendering assistance to the needful students. Such benevolent deed can be performed by only the teachers who are retiring from the teaching profession, which is not found in other professions.

The post-retirement activities of an employee reflect the disposition of the person concerned. Accordingly, the post-retirement activities also have the same importance. On the basis of the post-retirement activities it can be stated that with how much sincerity and ability the employee concerned might have discharged his duty during the tenure of service. The society accepts him as a life-long teacher, which is not found in other professions. Even after retirement the teacher who engages himself in the activities befitting a teacher can be affirmed that he has passed his life as the teacher in the true sense of the term.

A specific characteristic – devotion to the concerned institution – was commonly observed in the teachers who were working in good institutions. Good institutions are instrumental in making good teachers and good teachers contribute to rendering good institution. In view of this, good (and true) teachers spend most of their time and energy only for the school. Viewed in this context, good and true teachers spend their maximum time and energy only for the school. Naturally, the post-retirement activities of such teachers must be devoted to the welfare of their families or the society, as a token for the reward of the obligation done to them by the family as well as the society. For rendering useful service, they should be careful to keep themselves healthy.

It is often observed that some persons might have grown old but not deserving persons. The sooner they retire the better it would be for the fields of education and society. But alas, such a situation is rarely seen! At the time of getting retired as a teacher, he should sincerely ask himself, "Have I set an exemplary behaviour for the students?" If the answer is "yes" (then) you are successful as a teacher; otherwise not. The teacher who has not become a role model for the students (or say, even for one student!), his life (or career) as a teacher can be said to have been utterly useless. The teacher has not to work for salary only; he has to work with emotions and sympathy for the learners. If there is joy wherever the teacher goes, (then) he is the successful teacher. And if there is joy when he leaves the job, (then) he is the unsuccessful teacher.

Note:

- *The teacher who has not become a role model for the students in his career, his life is utterly useless.*
- *The teacher has not to work for salary only; he has to work with emotions and sympathy for the learners.*

21

A TEACHER HAS TO BECOME A ROLE MODEL

*I*n a prayer assembly in Education college, a lady student-teacher (trainee) spoke on 'Effort'. Whatever she spoke, it was not in fact, spoken; but she read it out loudly. The writer who was present could not help remain silent, but he remarked, "Now that you have spoken on 'Effort', I would like to ask you: "How much effort you have made in preparing the script to help you to speak here personally?" Thus it is easy to advise others, but difficult to act accordingly. Everybody has the habit to advise others, irrespective of whether he is educated or illiterate. Even the teacher is not an exception. In a way to give advice is considered to be the teacher's duty. If it is based on the realistic foundation, it is taken as proper advice. The teachers, who advise others or to whom the others approach for advice, themselves hesitate to accept such advice in their own cases.

A research on 'Teachers' children's study: Nature and present status' needs to be undertaken. After having accepted the teacher's job, he is generally found engrossed in private tuitions. He cannot spare even an hour for teaching his child at home. Having amassed lacs of rupees by way of tuitions, he has to donate a huge amount in lacs of rupees for his children's higher studies. Thus being mad after private tuitions as the cost of his children's study, he has finally to suffer a great financial loss. Does the teacher fulfil his children's expectations as the parent himself while expecting other parents to do so?

How about the teacher who rebukes the late comer in the classroom, himself entering the classroom late? The teacher's verbally taught values would be effective only when he himself maintains them. The teacher himself should try to be exemplary in behaviour rather than a preacher. Preaching involves telling, whereas setting an example involves acting, or behaving oneself. Doing or behaving is more effective than telling. The students not only listen to teachers but they observe the teacher's behaviour also. Let the teachers believe that the students do not observer their behaviour. Alas, the students not only mark their behaviour but they criticize it also. The teacher's every aspect of behaviour is discussed by: the primary school children with their parents; by the secondary school students among their friend circles and at the college stage, the students do so in the entire community.

In this way the students act as media of propaganda of the teachers' work, behaviour or thinking. If the teachers want to transform the media of propaganda in their favour, the good words alone would not do; they should do something substantial that would deserve their respect. This is not a difficult task for the teachers to achieve. They are the most trustworthy persons by the students. This trust should, anyhow, be sustained. In support of this, two illustrations are cited.

A twelve-year student of Class Six, though sick, refused to take medicine. The parent tried to persuade and even threatened, but of no avail; the child was firm. At last his mother requested his teacher to come and persuade him. She told the teacher that if he personally asked the child to take medicine, he would definitely take it. The teacher lovingly persuaded the child to take the medicine. And lo! The child began to take it! The other case is of a bridegroom going for marriage (with the bride) along with the marriage party. The writer accompanied them. For one reason or the other, the bridegroom felt offended and refused to marry. All efforts to persuade him by the guardian and relatives failed. At last the bridegroom's father approached the writer (who happened to be the college professor) to persuade the bridegroom to marry. Regardless of the bridegroom's arguments, he lovingly asked him to sit at the marriage place. He bowed down to the writer and smilingly sat down for marriage. To cite another instance, a past student-teacher was ready to give divorce to his wife only after four months of marriage. The author called him personally and persuaded him not to do so. He agreed and now even after twelve years, the couple is living happily together.

The instances cited above are not for self praise; they are meant to ensure the readers that if the students have love and respect for the teacher, they can do anything and everything for them. They give you respect only when you have become an ideal for them. (In view of the author) the teacher who could not become a role-model for even five students during the tenure of his service for thirty years or so, does not deserve pension. Even today many retired persons or persons in service remember their teachers with respect, and discuss how impressive they were in teaching as well as in their behaviour with students. The opportunity to earn such liveliness is difficult in other professions. That is why the teacher's profession is the loftiest profession.

Note:

- Does the teacher fulfil his children's expectations as the parent himself while expecting other parents to do so?
- The students not only listen to teachers but they observe the teacher's behaviour also.

22

WE ARE TEACHERS LET US DO THIS MUCH

*T*he writer who is a Professor of Education had an occasion to go to the Academic staff college to deliver a lecture before the lecturers of Gujarat University Colleges during their orientation course. The majority of the male and female lecturers were young. The discourse with them was very lively. The strong desire and enthusiasm to accomplish something substantial was clearly evident in them. Some sort of disappointment was also visible on their faces for the non-fulfilment of some expectations from society or the government. On the whole, they were found fully confident. The discussion with such optimistic lecturers proved to be very fruitful. Given below are the suggestions given to them to become successful teachers as well as the importance shown to them about educative values.

The teacher's work in the classroom is not to give only information. If, through education, only information or knowledge has to be given, it is not necessary to spend crores of rupees in erecting school or college buildings. Information-giving can be done by parent, neighbour or even tuition classes. Really speaking, the teacher's job is to develop various skills in students along with their cultural development.

In writer's opinion, the present-day student seems to possess more information (or knowledge) compared to the teacher. The teacher has the knowledge of the subject that he teaches, whereas the student has the knowledge of the seven subjects that he is learning. Today's student collects heaps of knowledge and information through the internet. He is now habituated to get all that information he desires to have through the internet. Hence to become a successful teacher, make the internet your close friend. Every teacher must possess an internet connection at home, and it must be regularly operated also. The useful and relevant information should be utilised during the classroom transaction also. At present there might be many such high school or college students who might have their own blog. Hence the teachers also should make their own blogs. If they fail to do so, they would be blocked. At present every teacher must develop a habit of surfing for two-three hours on an average every day. Keeping himself informed with up to date information would help him remain more progressive compared to the students.

It is a general impression that the teacher intending to teach new things is usually found teaching old matters. To become a successful teacher, he shall have to abandon old matter. No matter the subject matter for teaching may be in accordance with the curriculum, if the teacher renovates it by bringing diversity and depth every year, the learners as well as teachers will experience freshness. The teaching-learning process is not the process of brain only, but it is also the process of heart. Therefore, during the process of teaching, the teacher should use not only the brain but the heart also. His teaching should be emotive also. He should be a model teacher.

The teacher should not be an atheist; he should be a theist. This means he should have faith. He should have faith chiefly on three aspects: on himself, on his work and on his students. If you do not have faith on your own self, how would other persons have faith on you? Similarly, if you do not repose on students, how would they repose on you? Every teacher must bear in mind that the teacher's job is not limited to making others listen to him, but he has to listen to others as well. As of now, several teachers complain that the students do not listen to them at all. It is evident that if you listen to them as teachers, they would, of course, listen to you as students. Every teacher should bear in mind that besides listening, the student has something to tell or ask him also. That teacher is a better teacher who teaches by doing rather than by speaking. He is the best teacher who inspires the students to learn by doing. Thus, the teacher of today needs to transform himself. Let the teacher come out of the rut: I alone should speak; I alone should do. Let the student speak more, do more. This done, both the sides would benefit. This would result in good development of the student, and the teacher would get some rest and keep himself ever fresh.

Just a warning! Kindly see to it that in doing so only the cognitive relation between the teacher and the students is not established. To become a successful teacher the affective relationship with the students should also be maintained. Besides the students, he should listen to their parents (or guardians) also. They have unparalleled faith for the teacher. Hence it is the teacher's duty to fulfil their expectations.

The writer (referred to as the Professor of Education at the outset) exhorts the teachers on three points (1) You must be remembering some of your teachers positively even today with respect and positive feelings for their merits and good qualities. Try to emulate them. (2) You must have come across even such teachers for whom you must have no respect or good feelings because of their vices. In case you have such vices, kindly try to shun them. (3) What are your expectations from your child's teacher? Think awhile. Do you as teachers fulfil such expectations? If you ponder (over) these three cases sincerely and try to put them into practice, nothing more is required to become a successful teacher.

Note:

- *To become a successful teacher, he shall have to abandon old matter.*
- *Let the teacher come out of the rut: I alone should speak; I alone should do.*

23

FOR THE IMPROVEMENT OF THE TEACHER THE SOCIETY NEEDS TO IMPROVE ITSELF

Today the society views the teacher with suspicion. The society is not satisfied with the teacher's behaviour or his role. Besides this, it throws blame or responsibility on him for his negative behaviour. It leaves no stone unturned in defaming the teacher. The question arises as to who is more responsible for such incidence. The teacher has lost that status and reputation that he enjoyed long ago.

Some time back the teacher enjoyed unparalleled respect in society. He used to be considered more ideal than even chief of the village. He enjoyed respect from the elders or the aged persons assembled at the central place of the village. The teacher's role in resolving quarrels in the village was unparalleled. It was not unusual to see quarrelling persons pausing for two minutes as a mark of respect for the teacher. The teacher was found to be neutral in settling the dispute. He considered himself indebted to the society. He was always trying to give solace or comfort to the pupil for alleviating his trouble by placing or moving his hand on the pupil's head. Now the question arises: How is it that the distance between the society and the teacher has been increasing? What is wrong between the two? Society or community is the collection or the group of people. What sort of the behaviour patterns of the members of the society (barring teachers) are such as would increase the distance between the teacher and the community? In this regard, a few instances are cited here.

In the society vices are increasing, magnitude of crimes is also on the increase. The present society itself seems to be polluting and it expects the teacher to improve! When the vice in the form of corruption is pervading in the society, hardly some teacher might have remained unaffected. Think just a while that the teacher not intending to give bribe requires giving bribe helplessly. What would have been his mental condition? What would be his image of the children's parents in view of such a situation? Would it not have any effect on his vision about the children?

Despite this, we advise that the teacher should refrain himself from such misconduct. When the fraudulent tricks, vices and destruction or deterioration of value system is rampant in society, how could we expect the teacher remaining unaffected? He is also a member of the society! Every member of the society including the teacher cannot remain unaffected. Despite this, the society (community) exhorts only the teachers to improve.

The teacher himself never wishes to do wrong. He does not have even the courage to do wrong. In spite of this, the members of the society press him to do wrong, especially during the examination period of time. During the class-room teaching, the teacher sometimes gives some punishment to the student. The guardian feels annoyed and lodges a complaint at the police station! What sort of feelings for the teacher might have directed him to do so? Have we ever heard of the teachers getting together in case of the guardian's common mistake? Does this fact not reflect the teacher's magnanimity? If required, the teacher at times invites Government's his displeasure also when he fights for the students' interest! Is there any instance of the guardian having written even a letter to the Government for the teachers' welfare? Despite this, the majority of the teachers sincerely remains connected with the community (society), and tries their best for the improvement and welfare of the society. It is the irony of fate that the society exhorts the teachers to improve!

About a century back, when a teacher approached the shopkeeper to purchase some commodity, the shopkeeper would give him the same with a smile on his face; at times he would forgo the amount! Contrary to this, today's community is not at all prepared to give the teacher anything on credit. It was so to say customary to give the crop from the field to the teacher gratis with affection. Those were the days when the guardian (or parent) never expected the teacher to declare the son/daughter successful at the examination (irrespective of merit). The members of the then society had boundless respect for the teacher. Today, it seems that the teacher is so to say, made helpless and downgraded, (in author's view). (The author attributes it to the society or community). It is feared that thousands of the sincere teachers might lose their vitality or even sincerity in such an unsympathetic society! The teacher had been good in the past; is good at present and he sincerely wants to remain good for ever. He simply needs the encouragement from the community (or society as such). The negative response from the community tends to produce inferiority in teachers. In fact, it is the society (or community) that needs to improve itself; the teacher would then improve himself easily. Even today, many teachers maintain their sincerity undisturbed against the ill-treatment by the community. Let the community (or society) discharge its duty very well. The teacher will follow suit. Let the society fully and sincerely respect the teacher, trust him and sincerely love him. Then see how sincerely he loves and takes care of your children!.

Note:

- *The teacher himself never wishes to do wrong.*
- *The negative response from the community tends to produce inferiority in teachers.*

24

EDUCATIONAL WORK AS WORSHIP

*E*veryone is busy at any moment. When we ask what is going on. The answer is just nothing; sitting at leisure. In fact that person does the work of sitting idly. In other words man has the power of thoughts. He goes on thinking every moment. If you think to pass a few moments without thinking, it is highly impossible for a common person. Thoughtless person hardly meets the success. Thoughts should be positive and practical. A person takes up the task at the end of thinking or continues thinking while doing the work. Sometimes expected things happen and we call it a success and if it does not happen so, we call it failure.

A teacher has to work with the children. Sometimes the children hardly reach the expected learning goal; hence he becomes upset. In case of repeated failure, the teacher leaves his efforts. Moreover the teacher's task is not limited to the classroom. More educational and social duties are to be performed by them. If satisfaction is to be had, work should be considered as worship. In case of failure, there will be real satisfaction without despair. This implies not only to the teacher but to every vocation. Let us understand how the work of teaching is accepted as worship just as we remember the moments of our worship to our gods.

Worship to Lord is a spiritual matter. It is highly pious so as the work of teaching is pious and there should be the addition of spirituality. When we start worshipping our Lord, we do it single-mindedly. In the same way the teacher, while doing any kind of teaching, should do it with integration. We hope to get something from the Lord in our worship. But we may not get whatever we desire. Yet we hardly blame on him. The next day we again get ready to worship whole-heartedly. In the same way if the teacher does not succeed, he should never blame his fate or his students; but the next day he must continue the same process with full trust and sincerity. Worship helps in getting self satisfaction and self confidence. When the teacher looks at his work as worship, he would increase his self confidence and self satisfaction. An idler hardly gets satisfaction. When worship is performed whole-heartedly; it brings about expected results. So the teacher must do his job of teaching whole heartedly and with full trust. There is the attribute of devotion in our worship. There is firm belief in devotion. Sometimes true belief changes into misbelieve. The teacher has to notice this misbelieve. As the worshipper trust on his God, the teacher has to trust on his students. During worship whatever desire or result is expected, may not be achieved soon, yet the same must continue the very next day. The teacher should also continue his task if the expected result is not achieved soon after the task of teaching. Doing so, he will never get tired and never get over burdened by this work. If we never compromise or adjust our ceremony of worship during the time of dawn or dusk; why should the teacher, to compromise with the ceremony of teaching and time? As regular worship is done, the same regularity must be followed in educational work. Regularity shows the devotion to work. Worship is performed with utter devotion and with unique oneness and even with the forgetfulness of the surrounding world. In the same way the teacher has to do his job with total interest and full trust. As we never distrust our Lord in our worship and perform it with all the articles and aids like the lamps and scent sticks, the teacher should also enter the classroom with sufficient aids to perform his educational task. Just as the place of worship is considered a temple, the classroom should be also considered to be a temple. The photo frame of the picture of our Lord is lifeless. And yet how much honour is paid! We take the picture to be our Lord and take care of it. The students sitting before the teacher are full of life, hence the teacher has to take care of them and honour them. How often does a person remember his Lord in a day? Your answer is: many a times. In the same way the teacher has not to forget his students consciously and remember them constantly. Any person tries to please the Lord with as many efforts as are to be done by the teacher to please his students! To perform worship is a religious task. Thus with the utter devotion and trust, kept in the religious work, the same should be followed by the teacher in his educational work. Thus let all the teachers be theist as is expected!

Note:

- *Worship helps in getting self satisfaction and self confidence.*
- *If the teacher does not succeed, he should never blame his fate or his students.*

25

TEACHER'S RESPECT IN THE PAST, TODAY AND IN THE FUTURE

Every year September 5 is celebrated as the Teachers' Day. The main objectives of the Teachers' Day celebration are: to acknowledge unparalleled importance of the teacher for the society; to recognise the teacher's role as dignified and thus to honour him. Fifth day of September, the birthday of the first President of the Republic of India Dr. Sarvapalli Radhakrishnan is being celebrated in India as the Teachers' Day since 1962. In the whole world, the World Teachers' Day is celebrated on the Fifth October every year since 1994. To eulogize the teacher's role, the State as well as the Central Governments honours the outstanding teachers every year. Several social and educational institutions also have begun to honour the deserving teachers. The teachers and the soldiers are the important human forces for the development and security of any nation. The nation whose teachers are devoid of strength can never achieve progress, and whose army is weak can never sleep peacefully.

The teacher's role is of great importance for any society or nation. Chanakya, the renowned economist (and teacher) of ancient India, had declared, "The teacher is never ordinary…" The ages back, the teacher's role had been acclaimed as important, it is so important at present and will remain significant even after years in future also. (In this connection, the writer who happens to be the Professor of Education in S.U.G. College of Education for Bachelor's Degree of Education in Ahmedabad cites his experience with around eighty student-teachers (trainee).

The Professor asked the student-teachers a pinpointed question: Why do you want to become a teacher? Give me your reply on a piece of paper. The pattern of their responses is given below in their own words.

- In the teacher's profession we get more joy and freedom.
- The teacher is best, compared to other employees.
- The country can be directed in a specific direction.
- Even the Chief Minister may address him as 'Sir'.
- It is the teacher's job where you get more respect.
- I want to become teacher so as to remove faults and vices from the society.
- To build up a good society.
- To give good knowledge and to become knowledgeable.
- In teacher's job, our fondness or hobby can be satisfied with good salary.
- We forget our troubles so long as we are in company with the students.
- To impart that type of good education which we could not receive.
- To eliminate corruption.

- To obtain good status.
- To teach the students the subject of his interest.
- Next to the parents the teacher's status is high.
- To impart knowledge to the illiterate persons and educate them.
- It is pleasurable to teach children.
- To eliminate illiteracy and blind faith.
- To quicken the self-development.
- To give good and true guidance to the members of my family.
- Inspired from my teacher, I want to become a teacher.
- For women the teacher's job is better than any other job.
- To see, to know and to enjoy the innocence, by working in company with the children.
- To empower India's future.
- To fulfil the dream cherished in adolescence to become a teacher.
- Having studied Arts subjects no other job except the teacher's job can be obtained.
- To impart knowledge more than the bookish knowledge.

It was joyful to know such positive and joyous thoughts of the student-teachers. There are many reasons for being delighted. First, the student-teachers have full faith in teaching profession. This faith itself will make them successful. They know and they accept too that the teachers' social status is remarkable and dignified in many ways. This belief itself will sustain them in this profession and help them to succeed in it. Their vision was distinct. They want to enjoy working with children and helping them to learn.

From this viewpoint, it is clear that the teacher's importance had been recognised in the past, is being accepted at present and will also be sustained in future.

Note:

- *The nation whose teachers are devoid of strength can never achieve progress, and whose army is weak can never sleep peacefully.*
- *The teacher's importance had been recognised in the past, is being accepted at present and will also be sustained in future.*

26

TEACHERS' IMAGES ARE REFLECTED IN THE STAFFROOM

The schools and colleges look beautiful because of their diverse aspects or some particular aspects. For instance library, laboratory, drawing room, prayer hall, playground, the Principal's chamber and so on. Sometimes it is heard that a particular school or college has an extraordinary laboratory; the library and the reading room of a particular school or college are very much enriched; and also if you wish to enjoy the prayer programme, do visit that particular school; that particular school makes abundant use of its school ground and so on. Here the other aspect of the school also needs to be added and that is its staff room. With regard to the academic environment, the staff room plays an important role. The policy and the conduct of the school or college are usually discussed in the staffroom, or sometime given shape also, not withstanding this, the writer is shocked to see the environment of the staff rooms of various schools.

Since the writer happens to be the Professor of a college of teacher-education, he has occasions to go to many schools. There he usually spends some time in the staffroom with the teachers, where he has glimpse of the nature of the institution and its future. Some time it is heard that the particular institution is a very old institution. Formerly it was a hard task for the parents to get their sons/ daughters' admission there. All the classes were fully occupied. But alas! Today the strength of the students has dwindled extremely. One would like to ask, "How is it so?" Out of many factors responsible for such a downfall, one is the teaching staff of the school. The emotional environment of the staff-room greatly influences the sincerity, fervour, policy and the style of teaching staff. The staff can upgrade or ever downgrade any newly appointed teacher.

The writer reports that he had an occasion to spend around ten minutes in the staffroom of a school where he overheard some discussion that was giving on. It was related mainly to the investment of money as to whether it should be invested in Share market or in purchasing land. Some teachers seated in another corner were busy discussing some particular marriage occasion.

The staffroom was not the place suitable for such discussions. At different occasions, in different schools, the subject-matter of the different staffrooms discussion is found to be varying. But alas! The subject-matter of the staff-room discussion is related mainly to any aspect except teaching or education. In such schools there may be one or two friends who might not be interested in such matters as related to earlier. The poor fellows are not in a position to stop them talking on matters not related to education. They may even leave the staff-room and take seat outside. In some schools, the doors of the staffroom were found closed so as to avoid their discussion being overheard! The students' classroom is just adjoining the staffroom. It means there is extreme noise in the staffroom. How can such teachers ask the noise-making students to stop doing so in the classroom? Can such teachers be meted out with any sort of the usual punishments given to the students who misbehave in the classroom?

The staffroom is an important place which is instrumental in formulating the policy and method of the working of the school as well as the classroom transaction. The discussions held there must be positive and educational. The staff-room is the staff's mirror from where the reflected image of the staff is observed. Hence the discussions carried out in the staffroom must pertain to the subjects like education, parents, students, community, state or nation. The staffroom environment must be such where the teacher becomes fresh; and where the students and the guardians enter smilingly and go back also with the pleasing face. There is no place for uproar. Some teachers would like to read some magazines or books, but they do not find atmosphere congenial for reading. An Education officer who was on a visit to a reputed school of Ahmedabad noticed some teachers reading daily newspapers and periodicals in the staffroom. He suggested that daily newspapers and periodicals should be placed only in the library. The teachers may go there for reading. The purpose behind his suggestion was that the teacher may read reference literature for his subject in the staffroom and may read other literature in the library. The result was that the teachers stopped extra reading altogether.

In a way, if we want to stop discussions on other subjects in the staff-room, let the reading material of the teachers' interest enter the staff-room. This would automatically stop or reduce making fun and cracking jokes. When it is found that the teachers are more interested in reading, more useful reading material can be provided. First, make the teacher read, thereafter change the reading material and replace it by more useful literature. Once the teacher starts reading, turn him towards reading suitable and useful books and magazines. This would ultimately result into a positive change into the discussion of the subject-matter in the classroom, besides that in the staffroom. The discussions carried out in the staffroom must be respected to the same extent as those undertaken at home. Try to keep the staffroom as clean and beautiful as the residence. In short, the staffroom is such a place which influences the educational and emotional environment of the academic institutions like schools and colleges. Amen!

Note:

- *The staffroom is an important place which is instrumental in formulating the policy and method of the working of the school as well as the classroom transaction.*
- *Try to keep the staffroom as clean and beautiful as the residence.*